refresh

CONTEMPORARY VEGAN RECIPES FROM THE AWARD-WINNING FRESH RESTAURANTS

Ruth Tal

with Jennifer Houston

Collins
An Imprint of HarperCollins*Publishers*

D1415990

Published by Collins, an imprint of HarperCollins Publishers Ltd.

Originally published by John Wiley & Sons Canada, Ltd.,
in both print and EPub editions: 2007

First published by Collins in this trade paperback edition and in an EPub edition: 2013

HarperCollins books may be purchased for educational, business, or sales
promotional use through our Special Markets Department.

HarperCollins Publishers Ltd
2 Bloor Street East, 20th Floor
Toronto, Ontario, Canada
M4W 1A8

www.harpercollins.ca

Library and Archives Canada Cataloguing in Publication information is available upon request

ISBN: 978-1-44342-946-7

Printed and bound in Canada
DWF 9 8 7 6 5 4 3 2 1

Cover and interior food photography, back cover and interior author photography: Lorella Zanetti
Front cover and interior restaurant photography (Spadina and Bloor locations): Andrej Kopac
Interior restaurant photography (Crawford location): Interior Images

For my sweet parents, Vered and David—
because you gave me the strength and independence to be myself
And then you found the courage to let me go

> Jennifer and Ruth

Acknowledgements

First, we would like to thank all our Fresh customers who, over the past 15 years, have supported and encouraged us with their daily presence, enthusiasm, feedback and positive energy. You make us all want to try harder, go further and do better every day. We are also indebted to our free-spirited staff of past and present for their hard work, dedication and support, all of which have helped make Fresh so unique and successful.

I would like to express my heartfelt gratitude to my Fresh family of business partners, Barry Alper and Jennifer Houston. With all this talk of good health, I am proud and delighted that we have one of the healthiest and most enjoyable partnerships around.

Thank you, Jennifer, for developing and refining the wonderful recipes in this cookbook. Your creativity, wit and perseverance have consistently elevated the Fresh kitchens to a higher level of presentation and taste. And your proofreading skills are unmatched in the Western world.

I would also like to thank the sparkling Jennifer Smith and Leah Fairbank at Wiley for believing in the magic we know as Fresh. Thank you for spearheading the move to launch a second edition of this beloved cookbook and for conjuring up the perfect title: *refresh*.

The following authors and their informative books have influenced me, and I have great respect for their integrity and scope of knowledge: Sam Graci, Harvey Diamond, Daniel J. Gagnon, Cherie Calbom, Norman W. Walker, Steve Meyerowitz, Ann Wigmore, John Robbins, Paul Pitchford, Michael Murray N.D., Anna Lappé, Bryan Terry and Ann Gentry.

Over the past year we have opened two new beautiful locations with the help of this talented team: Ralph Giannone and Brie Gillespie of Giannone Associates Architects Inc., Paul Syme and Bryan Jin of 3rd Uncle Design Inc., Orest Boszko of Boszko and Verity Inc., Morris Ortolan, Nigel Churcher of Genkey Design Ltd., Howard Dinetz of Dinetz Restaurant Equipment Ltd., Remo Alberico of Remco Mechanical, George De Francesca of Derok Electric and Marcus Grossman, our painter extraordinaire.

Thank you to my spicy family whose patience I continue to test and whose love I have always felt: David and Vered, Ronnie and Vicky, Iris and Michael. And also to my tribe of fantastic, fun-loving nieces and nephews: Adam, Adina, Ari, Carly, Jeremy, Jonah, Leah, Naftali, Shalom and Yoel.

My life is filled with the delightful presence of Bee and Rufus Churcher, Jaclyn Churcher, Stephanie, Chris, Lyndsay and Nigel Eyton. Thank you for embracing me with your warmth, acceptance and good humour from the very first moment we met. I enjoy you all so much.

Thank you to my generous family of friends: Lisa Kelner, Bonnie Beecher, Robyn Levy, Diane Bruni, Jane Loney, Jane Miller, Wende Cartwright, Alison Owen, Rhonda Moscoe, Jane Clapp, Kim Donnelly, Paul Austerberry, Debra Berman, Cyril Kaye, Pheona Wright, Anita Mancuso, Alan Thomson and Carlo Rota. And a big hug to my neighbourly neighbours, Don, Beth, Claire and Patsy Baker.

Finally, Nigel, I would like to thank you for lending your expertise and support to everything I do.

> Fresh on Crawford

> Fresh on Crawford

fresh
by JuiceForLife

modern food and juice

> Fresh on Spadina

Table of Contents

Looking Back, Moving Forward

Seven years ago, when this cookbook was first published, the word "vegan" was on the fringe, often mispronounced and possibly alluding to a cult. I was encouraged not to use the word in the title. Today, our customer is savvier. The average person seems to know more about healthier eating, possessing a voracious curiosity and a willingness to try new things. This is a refreshing change from the days when potential customers would read the menu, get up and back out the door, apologizing that it's just too healthy for them. These days, I often learn about popular dietary trends and nutritional supplements from our customers, who are constantly in search of new avenues to improved health and wellness.

The negative stereotypes associated with a vegan diet (undernourished, protein-deficient hippies and boring, bland health foods) have mostly disappeared. Yoga, meditation, naturopathy and acupuncture are booming along with natural food stores, organic produce, vegetarian restaurants and juice bars. Popular healing techniques, such as Ayurvedic medicine, that treat the body and mind as equal partners in wellness have led to a wider acceptance of alternative paths to better health. In addition, people everywhere are taking responsibility for their own health.

Shelves are bursting with choice for hungry but discerning natural food lovers with assorted food sensitivities. Grocery shopping has never been so exciting! I remember vividly, while on a trip in the U.S., having a near meltdown as I hungrily wandered the packed grocery aisles, searching for something I could eat that didn't have wheat, sugar, corn, yeast, preservatives, transfats or MSG. We want to eat in a way that is sustainable not only to the environment but also to ourselves and our bodies, and trends supporting this style of living are popping up everywhere. Currently, the hot new ingredients are maca protein, E3 Live, matcha green tea, kombucha, goji berries, pomegranate juice, acai berries and pure dark cacao nibs. Witness the appearance of these ingredients on the shelves in cereals, bulk bins, cookies, teas, tinctures and in juice bars and cafés. Of emerging interest is the raw food diet, the 100-mile diet, high-protein/low-carbohydrate diets and slow-cooked foods. Shade-grown, fair-trade organic espresso, organic milks and natural sweeteners are in high demand at local coffee joints.

My dream all along has been to get more people to believe that it's hip to be healthy, that having a healthy natural glow, exercising, relaxing and eating right for yourself and the planet could be the new definition of modern, trendy and cool. Being proud of our poor eating habits used to be a badge of honour; now it's so uncool.

Obviously, we are all different with varying lifestyles, habits, preferences and dislikes. What works well for one soul may not work for another. One thing is sure though: we all want to feel good, have more energy, enjoy life and live longer. Today, modern conventional Western medicine openly promotes eating a more plant-based diet to get the essential vitamins, minerals, antioxidants and phytochemicals we need. These nutrients help fight cancer, heart disease and many other ailments in our bodies, while nourishing and invigorating our lives. It is no longer considered alternative to understand these things to be true.

I know that there is no one perfect way to eat for everyone. Everyone must find his or her own balance, and that balance will always be in a state of flux. My own choices shift from time to time, depending on what I've read, what someone has told me and how I feel on any given day. Eating fresh, colourful, living foods will always be the mainstay of my diet, and yet as I evolve I find I want to remain open to new discoveries and be able to put them into practice, if they feel right. Like everyone else, I want to feel good. When I do, I find I am kinder to those around me and I have more time and energy to care about what I do and how it affects the earth. Taking that one step further, I know that eating an organic, plant-based diet, low on the food chain and free of animal products, is one way to make an enormous difference each and every day. Being healthy is never just one thing, one fix. It's everything we do and think, in balance, in harmony and with ease.

With three restaurants up and running and more on the way, we've grown from contributing to a niche market to being a popular award-winning destination in a booming industry. Since the *Juice for Life* cookbook came out in 2000 our business has matured and grown. We changed our name to Fresh, indicating our shift in emphasis from a juice bar to a vegetarian restaurant whose basis is fresh imaginative recipes, ingredients and ideas. We wrote a second national best-selling cookbook, *Fresh at Home*. Finally, we moved and improved the two original locations and added a third. All three are beautiful, modern, architecturally designed spaces. Fresh on Crawford, our new addition in the trio, has won numerous international, national and local architectural and design awards. Fresh on Spadina is located in the fashion district, just south of Queen St. West. It is a modern urban space designed to feed with speed our many hungry patrons on their lunch and dinner breaks. Fresh on Bloor is located at the corner of Bloor and Spadina, on the northern edge of the University of Toronto campus and the bohemian Annex neighbourhood. It is now our largest eat-in and take-away restaurant space. Each space has its own individual personality, look and neighbourhood feel. They are noisy, busy centres of warmth and nourishment.

I've always believed that if I could make vegan eating more accessible, then more people (even my parents!) would want to eat this way. Despite being referred to as a chain, which never fails to produce a shudder in me, at our heart we remain a bustling neighbourhood restaurant serving delicious, nutritious comfort food in a welcoming atmosphere.

At Fresh, our menu has been built on a foundation of whole grains, vegetables, sprouts, herbs and spices, legumes, nuts, seeds and soy products. They are high in unrefined carbohydrates and fibre while being naturally low in fat. From the beginning we have prepared our food from scratch right in the restaurant and have always chosen fresh, high-quality ingredients to work with. When you get up from the table after eating at Fresh, you aren't laden down. You're energized. Our popularity has only confirmed what I have felt all along: with imagination, flair and creativity vegan food is one of the most exciting cuisines emerging today.

Refresh is the official second edition of *Juice for Life: Modern Food and Luscious Juice*, which has sold more than 17,000 copies over seven years. When the publisher decided it was time to retire the original cookbook, I thought, what a great idea! Now I can bring this much-loved cookbook into the present. Before I could argue my point, the editors offered to include the word "vegan" in the title—a lovely indication of how times have changed. This time around, I am delighted to share the authorship of this book with Jennifer Houston, our wizard in the kitchens, head chef and business partner. Despite many exciting new juice recipes, you will see that the emphasis has shifted away from juicing, toward showcasing our food. We've included a selection of new recipes we have been dying to share with you. You will find new creations in the soups, starters, salads, rice bowls, sauces and dressings. New detailed information can also be found in the Juicing Tips, Juice Fasting and Buying a Juicer sections.

Thank you for giving me this wonderful opportunity once again.

Still taking life by the fruit,

Ruth Tal

Fresh on Bloor
326 Bloor St. West
(at Spadina)

Fresh on Spadina
147 Spadina Ave.
(at Richmond)

Fresh on Crawford
894 Queen St. West
(at Crawford)

Fresh Food

Our Approach

Imagine feasting on foods that please your taste buds while providing supreme fuel to energize your body and brain, and on decadent foods that tread softly on this earth while sparing the animals on the journey to your table. Modern food is positive, conscious, compassionate and subtle. Leave your dogma at the door. A love of food and pleasure is all you need to indulge in the Fresh way of cooking. An addictive feeling of well-being, energy and alertness will follow. Eating this way at home is easy, fun and entirely possible.

Dining, whether at home or at a restaurant, is the quintessential sensual experience, one that engages all five of our senses. How food looks, its texture and the way it feels in our mouths, the aroma and flavour of the food and lastly, the sounds we make eating, are the ultimate turn-ons. But what about how it feels in our bodies afterwards?

Fresh recipes consider the healthful qualities as much as they do the flavour and presentation of each dish. How you feel when you get up after your meal is of paramount importance. I encourage you to get to know your body and its relationship to the foods you eat. No matter where you are on your path to better health and self-knowledge, you will find the following recipes an enjoyable part of the journey.

All of the recipes in this cookbook are suitable for those who follow a vegan diet, with the exception of those that contain honey or royal jelly. (Strictly speaking, honey and royal jelly are animal by-products and are therefore not considered vegan by some.) People with food sensitivities and allergies also have plenty to choose from. What is a vegan diet? It is a choice of food that excludes all meat, fish, fowl, dairy or eggs. Cooking vegan may sound limiting, but it's actually downright liberating. Excluding the usual animal-based part of your meal frees up space on your plate for an infinite variety of colourful fruits, vegetables, legumes, grains, nuts, seeds, herbs and spices. The following innovative recipes will show you how to use these ingredients to make delicious appetizers, soups, entrées, salads, burgers, wraps, dressings, sauces and spreads as well as tasty and fortifying brunches.

Once you get familiar with the recipes, feel free to mix and match them to your taste. For example, the Marrakesh Curried Stew is great on its own, but it is also used as the filling for the Roti for Life.

Food Tips

Cooking should be joyful and stress-free. If you are happy and relaxed, the positive energy will trickle into every morsel of food you are preparing. Conversely, if you are angry or upset, that negative energy will slip into your food and may even give you and your guests indigestion. Never cook if you are in a bad mood. Wait until you feel better. It is always good to be aware of who is preparing your food and your relationship to them. Cooking food for another person to ingest is a very intimate act. Your thoughts, feelings and attitudes come through in the food. When a restaurant has great food, chances are that whoever is cooking in the kitchen is a positive person with the right attitude!

What a Kitchen Wants and Needs

Of all the equipment and tools a person can have in the kitchen, a food processor is probably the most useful. It will save you a lot of time and enable you to explore most recipes with ease. A blender is the next best thing, great for making dressings, sauces and puréeing. Other invaluable tools in the kitchen include a good sharp knife, cutting board, measuring cups, hand juicer for lemons, measuring spoons, vegetable peeler, grater, rolling pin, whisk, colander, mixing bowls, a heavy-bottomed frying pan, small and medium saucepans and a soup pot.

Filtered Water

Water, which makes up two-thirds of our body's mass, is a vital nutrient for us all. Many people make the effort to seek healthy clean food but neglect to seek water of similar quality. When you are preparing good food that lists water as an ingredient, consider using purified or filtered water. You will also find that filtered water tastes sweeter and tap water tends to have a dull metallic aftertaste. This is especially important for cooking grains, soups and sauces where the water is absorbed into the food.

Cooking Grains

Brown rice takes a little longer to cook than white rice as the water has to penetrate the outer husk or bran. For a sweet toasted flavour, stir the rice in a dry saucepan first on medium to high heat for 2 minutes. I like to add a few slices of ginger root or garlic to the pot of rice as it's cooking for a subtle hint of flavour.

Brown Basmati or Other Long-Grain Rice

3 cups	**brown basmati or other long-grain rice**
5 cups	**filtered water**

Rinse the rice in a saucepan and drain. Add the water and bring to a boil; then reduce to a simmer and cook, covered, for 30 to 35 minutes, until water has evaporated. Makes 6 cups.

Sweet brown rice is a sticky rice, rich in gluten and protein, which we use for the Nori Roll (see page 48) and also for sushi. Adding the umeboshi, rice vinegar and maple syrup gives the rice a special hidden flavour. Umeboshi plum paste is available in Japanese and natural food stores.

Sweet Brown Rice

1 cup	**sweet brown rice**
1 1/2 cups	**filtered water**
1 tsp.	**rice vinegar (optional)**
1 tsp.	**maple syrup (optional)**
1 tsp.	**umeboshi plum paste (optional)**

Rinse the rice in a saucepan and drain. Add the water and bring to a boil, then reduce to a simmer and cook, covered, for 30 minutes or until all the water has evaporated. Combine the rice vinegar, maple syrup and umeboshi together in a small bowl and toss with the cooked rice. Makes 2 cups.

Cooking Beans

Beans or legumes are high in protein, fat and carbohydrates. They are also a rich source of potassium, calcium and iron. When sprouted, their valuable nutrients and enzymes increase even more. There are many beans to choose from, so if you have trouble digesting one kind, try another. To speed up cooking time and improve digestibility of the beans, soak them overnight in the fridge, for a minimum of 4 hours, in 3 parts water to 1 part beans. Drain the water and rinse the beans. Using canned beans is a practical option if you are short on time or energy. Choose beans that are packed in water with no salt.

Combine 1 cup of soaked beans with 3 cups of water and bring to a boil. Simmer for 1 1/2 to 2 hours. Cooking time decreases with the size of bean and length of time soaked—smaller beans and beans that have had a lengthy soak will have a shorter cooking time. Lentils and split peas are quicker to cook than larger beans; they take 30 to 40 minutes.

Toasted Nuts and Seeds

The mix of nuts and seeds below adds texture and flavour to salads, such as the Mega Life Salad (see page 40). Oil-rich nuts and seeds are one of the best sources of vitamin E, an antioxidant that strengthens the immune system and essential fatty acids. They are also an abundant source of protein and fat, which are best consumed in small portions. Light toasting cuts down on the oiliness, making nuts and seeds easier to digest. Overheating them, on the other hand, causes the fats and oils to be harmful to us. The healthful properties of nuts and seeds are greatly increased when they are chewed well.

1/4 cup	cashews
1/4 cup	walnuts
1/4 cup	sunflower seeds
2 tbsp.	flax seeds
1/8 cup	tamari (optional)
1/8 cup	maple syrup (optional)

Combine the nuts and seeds. Lay them on a flat pan and toast them in a 350-degree oven for about 45 minutes or until they are light brown. While toasting, toss the mixture a couple of times to prevent scorching. Store in a cool dry place.

To make trail mix, add 1/4 cup each of almonds, raisins and grated coconut.

Mixed Dry Herbs

This mix of dried herbs is used in the Herb Tofu Mayo (see page 102) and the Fresh Burger Mix (see page 58). You can also use it as an herbal shake for salads and rice dishes. Whenever possible, buy organic non-irradiated herbs that haven't been tampered with; they will generally have more flavour.

1 tbsp.	basil
1 tbsp.	oregano
1 tbsp.	thyme
1 tbsp.	marjoram
1 tbsp.	sage
1 tbsp.	tarragon

Mix all the herbs together and store in a glass jar in a cool dry place.

Toasting Spices

Toasting spices releases the locked-in flavours and greatly enhances the potency of the spice. This is one step in a recipe you don't want to miss. Toast the spices in a dry pan over medium heat, until the spices darken slightly and give off fragrant wisps of smoke. This usually takes no more than a couple of minutes. Remove spices from pan immediately.

Grinding Spices

Much like coffee beans, once a spice has been ground, its flavour and freshness diminish quickly. Buy whole spices and grind just the amount you need for your recipe for stronger flavour and aroma.

Date Purée

When baking, dates are a wonderful natural sweetener to replace sugar, honey or maple syrup. They build strength and are warming to the body. See Chocolate Chip Spelt Muffins (page 119) and Banana Muffins (page 120).

2 1/2 cups	cooking dates
2 1/2 cups	filtered water
1 tbsp.	vanilla extract
1/2 tsp.	cinnamon
1 pinch	nutmeg

Wash and rinse the dates. Put them in a saucepan with the water, vanilla extract, cinnamon and nutmeg. Cook on low heat for 25 minutes until half the water has evaporated. Remove from heat and let cool. When cool, place the date mixture in a food processor or blender and purée. Store in the fridge. Makes 2 cups.

Appetizers

Taking your time when you dine is an important part of good digestion. The first course sets the pace and tone for the entire meal. Served in small portions, an intensely flavoured dish will stimulate the appetite and get your juices flowing with anticipation of more. The following recipes, attractively arranged on platters, can double as delicious party treats or creative dishes for potluck dinners.

Coconut Tempeh (New!)

We created this crispy delectable appetizer in our search for creative new ways to offer tempeh. On our journey we happily discovered it also works well as a protein-rich topping for any rice bowl or salad. Try it with the Mango Cilantro Dipping Sauce (see page 88).

Serves 4

Ingredients

1 block	tempeh, cut into bite-sized chunks
2 cups	shredded coconut
1/4–1/2 cup	Canola oil
1 batch	Dosa Batter (see p. 11)

Marinade

2 cups	filtered water
2	bay leaves
1 tbsp.	garlic powder
2 tbsp.	sea salt

Method

1. Mix marinade ingredients in a small bowl and pour over cut tempeh. Let marinate at least 2 hours.
2. Put tempeh into a large bowl and discard marinade.
3. Pour dosa batter over tempeh and stir to coat each piece.
4. Lay out coconut on a baking sheet and coat each piece of tempeh with coconut, pressing it gently to make sure it sticks and the entire piece is covered.
5. Let tempeh sit in fridge for 30 minutes to set.
6. Heat oil in saucepan over medium heat and gently drop tempeh into oil. Cook until golden brown. Drain on paper towels and serve with a wedge of lime.

Indian Dosas

There are several steps to this recipe but don't be discouraged—the exotic flavour and presentation of this appetizer is worth it. These dosas can be served as a main course dish with a side of steamed rice and vegetables.

Serves 4

Ingredients

Dosa Pancakes

1 cup	**light spelt flour**
1/2 tsp.	**sea salt**
1/2 tsp.	**baking powder**
1/2 tsp.	**curry powder**
1/2 cup	**plain soymilk**
3/4 cup	**filtered water**
3 tbsp.	**sunflower oil**

Dosa Filling

1 batch	**Curried Garbanzo Filling (see p. 101), heated**

Dosa Toppings

1 batch	**Coconut Curry Sauce (see p. 86), heated**
1/4 cup	**grated coconut**
1/4	**cucumber, sliced**

Method

Dosa Pancakes

1. Combine Dosa Pancake dry ingredients in a bowl.
2. Gradually add soymilk and water and whisk until smooth.
3. Heat a portion of sunflower oil in a large flat-bottomed frying pan or griddle over medium heat. Add oil as needed.
4. Ladle 1 ounce of batter onto the hot surface in a circular motion until you have a thin, round pancake. Wait until bubbles appear and the surface no longer looks wet.
5. Flip the pancake over, cook for a few seconds and remove from heat.
6. Repeat to make 8 pancakes.

To Assemble the Dosas

1. Take 2 dosa pancakes and place 3 tablespoons of Curried Garbanzo Filling across the centre of each one. Roll them up, leaving the ends open.
2. Ladle a portion of warm Coconut Curry Sauce onto a plate. Place the two dosas on the plate of sauce.
3. Garnish with grated coconut and cucumber slices. Repeat for each serving.

Sweet Potato Wontons

We use pre-made spring roll wrappers, available at most Asian grocery stores, to make wontons. Regular wonton wrappers usually contain eggs.

Serves 6

Ingredients

2 tbsp.	olive oil
1	onion, peeled and diced
3 cloves	garlic, minced
1 tbsp.	store-bought yellow curry paste
2 tbsp.	tamari
1 tsp.	sea salt
1 tsp.	pepper
2 tsp.	raw sugar
1	sweet potato, peeled and shredded
1 tbsp.	grated coconut
1/2 cup	chopped scallions
1/2 cup	chopped cilantro or Thai basil
3 tbsp.	flour

Method

1. In a saucepan, sauté onion and garlic in olive oil until soft.
2. Add the yellow curry paste and cook for 1 minute.
3. In a small bowl, mix the tamari sauce, sea salt, pepper and raw sugar. Add these to the saucepan and stir.
4. Add the sweet potato and cook until soft, about 5 minutes. Add the remaining ingredients, except flour, and remove from heat.

To Assemble the Wontons

1. Take a package of thawed spring roll wrappers and separate each one, laying them on the counter for easy reach. Cover the pile with a damp cloth.
2. Combine flour and water to make a paste. This will act like a glue to keep the wontons together.
3. Take a wrapper, cut it in 4 squares and layer 2 squares on top of each other. Place 1 tablespoon of filling in the middle of each double-layered square. Spread the flour and water paste around the edge of the wrapper with a pastry brush or with your fingers. Fold wrapper around the filling, pinching all edges together to form a little package. Hold together for a few seconds until it sticks. Place each wonton on a cookie sheet. Repeat until you've used up all your filling.

To Cook the Wontons

1. Heat 1 cup of sunflower oil in a saucepan. You will need enough sunflower oil to cover the wontons by about 1/2 inch. Carefully drop wontons into the hot oil and cook until golden brown. Remove from oil and drain on a paper towel. Serve immediately with warm Garlic Dipping Sauce (see p. 88).
   If you don't want to fry the wontons, you can bake them in the oven at 400° F for 15 minutes or until the wrappers are crisp and starting to brown.

Mogan's Samosas

These samosas were created by Mogan, our Sri Lankan prep chef. This recipe is divided into three parts: the dough, the filling and the assembly. In all, samosas take about an hour and a half to make but they are well worth the effort. Try our Tahini Sauce (see page 98) for dipping. These samosas make a great party treat! These are not especially spicy samosas. Add a couple of pinches of cayenne pepper for more heat.

Makes 12 samosas

Ingredients

Samosa Filling

10 cups	filtered water
2	large potatoes, peeled and diced
2 tbsp.	olive oil
2	red onions, peeled and diced
1/4 cup	grated carrots
1/2 cup	frozen green peas
1/4 cup	chopped cilantro
6 tbsp.	Sri Lankan Spice Mix (see p. 94)
1 1/2 tsp.	sea salt

Samosa Dough

2 1/2 cups	durum flour
1/2 cup	white flour
1/2 cup	durum atta flour
1 1/2 tsp.	sea salt
1 tbsp.	sunflower oil
1 1/2 cups	warm filtered water

Method

Samosa Filling

1. Bring water to a boil in a large saucepan. Add potatoes and bring water back to a boil. Reduce to simmer. Cook until potatoes are soft. Drain.
2. In a frying pan, heat olive oil over medium heat. Add onions and cook for 5 minutes until soft. Add carrots, peas, cilantro and Sri Lankan Spice Mix. Stir to mix and continue cooking for 1 minute. Remove from heat.
3. In a large mixing bowl, combine the potatoes with the vegetable mixture. Add salt. Stir to mix thoroughly. Let cool.

Samosa Dough

1. In a large bowl, mix the dry ingredients.
2. In a measuring cup, mix the wet ingredients.
3. Form a well in the centre of the flour. Pour in the wet ingredients. Mix together, with your hands, until a dough forms.
4. Place dough onto a floured surface and knead for about a minute, until dough is smooth. Wrap in plastic and let sit for 1/2 hour.

To Assemble the Samosas

1. Make a paste with flour and water. This paste will help keep the samosas together.
2. Divide the dough into 12 equal portions. On a floured surface, roll each piece of dough into a circle about 6 inches in diameter. Fold the top eighth of each circle down to form a straight line.
3. Place approximately 1/3 cup filling on each circle of dough. Fold sides in to form a triangular package. Glue each surface together with flour paste.

To Cook the Samosas

Heat 1 cup sunflower oil in a deep pot over medium to high heat. Deep-fry samosas until golden brown. If you don't want to fry the samosas, brush them first with sunflower oil and bake them in the oven at 400° F for 15 minutes or until they start to brown.

Lucky Spring Rolls

We serve the Lucky Spring Rolls with our Garlic Dipping Sauce (see page 88). Pre-made spring roll wrappers can be bought at most Asian grocery stores or specialty food shops.

Makes 10 rolls

Ingredients

Spring Roll Filling

2 tbsp.	olive oil
1	onion, peeled and diced
6 cloves	garlic, minced
5 cups	sliced mushrooms
1 cup	shredded carrot
1 tbsp.	tamari
1 tsp.	raw sugar
1/2 tsp.	sea salt
1/2 tsp.	black pepper
1/4 package	rice vermicelli, soaked and cut in 1-inch pieces
1/2 cup	chopped scallions
1/2 cup	chopped cilantro
2 tbsp.	flour

Method

1. Heat olive oil in a saucepan over medium heat. Cook onion and garlic until soft.
2. Add mushrooms and carrot to the onion. Cook until most of the liquid released by the mushrooms has evaporated.
3. In a small bowl, mix the tamari, sugar, salt and pepper. Add to pan and cook for 1 minute.
4. Add soaked noodles and cook until softened, about 1 minute.
5. Add scallions and cilantro. Stir. Remove from heat. Let cool.

To Assemble the Spring Rolls

1. Take a package of spring roll wrappers and separate each one. Cover them with a damp cloth.
2. Make a paste with flour and water. This paste will help keep the spring rolls together.
3. Layer 2 wrappers on top of each other to create a double layer. Brush the points between the layers with flour paste.
4. Place 1/3 cup filling across the wrapper. Starting at a point, roll the wrapper firmly, folding the edges in as you go. Seal the top of the wrapper with flour paste and finish rolling.
5. Repeat for each spring roll.

To Cook the Spring Rolls

Heat 1 cup of sunflower oil on medium to high heat in a saucepan. Fry spring rolls until golden brown. They tend to float in the oil so you will have to hold them down under the oil. Instead of frying the spring rolls, you can bake them in the oven. Just brush the outside of the spring rolls with a little sunflower oil to keep them from getting too dry or cracking and bake at 400° F for 20 minutes.

Soups

Soup defines comfort food for me. Hearty, warm and filling, soup reminds me of home and family, when life was simple and slower paced. Nowadays, soup can be a quick meal-in-a-bowl for lunch or dinner, the first course of a leisurely dinner, or a mid-afternoon snack when you're hungry and it's too long to wait until dinnertime. I like to make my soup thick so I can pour it over a bowl of steamed rice or noodles. A soup can illuminate the very best special qualities of a certain fruit, vegetable or legume, such as the delicate sweetness of a pear, the fragrant aroma of red pepper, the velvety texture of butternut squash and the savoury flavour of black beans. Homemade soup is a great way to use whatever is at hand, and it's economical when you make large batches. These soups freeze nicely and taste even better the next day. The preparation time, once you have all the ingredients ready, is 20 to 30 minutes.

Vegetable Stock

A good vegetable stock can make all the difference between a decent soup and an amazing soup. This vegetable stock is easy to prepare. If you can spare the time, first roast the vegetables together in the oven before you simmer them on the stove. Store-bought vegetable stock in cubes or powder is a quick and easy option. These products can be found at most natural food stores.

Makes 10 cups

Ingredients

1	onion, peeled and chopped
1	carrot, peeled and chopped
1	tomato, chopped
1 cup	mushrooms
1 cup	parsley stems
5	garlic cloves, crushed
2 inches	ginger root
6	black peppercorns
1	bay leaf
10 cups	cold filtered water
	sea salt, to taste

Method

1. Put all the ingredients, except salt, in a large pot and cover with cold water. Simmer for 1 hour.
2. Strain stock through a fine-mesh sieve and discard the vegetables Add sea salt to taste.
3. Store in refrigerator or in the freezer.

Black Bean Passion Soup

This sultry soup has a spicy, smoky Southwestern flavouring. To speed up the preparation time for this soup, use canned black beans.

Serves 6

Ingredients

1 tbsp.	olive oil
1	onion, peeled and chopped
4 cloves	garlic, chopped
1/2 stalk	celery, chopped
3 medium	chipotle peppers, minced
4 cups	black beans, cooked
1 tsp.	white wine vinegar
1/2 tsp.	chili powder
1/4 tsp.	ground cloves
2 small	sweet potatoes, peeled and diced
2 tsp.	sea salt
1 1/2 tsp.	white pepper
6 cups	Vegetable Stock (see p. 20)

Method

1. Heat the olive oil over medium heat in a soup pot. Add the onion, garlic, celery and chipotle peppers. Sauté until soft.
2. Add the remaining ingredients and cover with vegetable stock.
3. Bring to a boil; then reduce to a simmer and cook for about 10 minutes until sweet potato is soft. Remove from heat.
4. Purée. Garnish with a sprig of cilantro or a slice of lime and serve.

Butternut Squash and Pear Soup

To enhance the wonderful pear flavour in the soup, leave the pear peel on. Yellow Bosc or green Anjou pears suit this soup well. Do not use overly ripe pears.

Serves 6

Ingredients

1 inch	ginger root, peeled and minced
1	cinnamon stick
1	butternut squash, peeled, seeded and diced
1	sweet potato, peeled and diced
6 cups	Vegetable Stock (see p. 20)
1 tbsp.	olive oil
1	onion, peeled and chopped
1/3 cup	white wine
2	pears, cored and sliced
1/2 cup	coconut milk
1 tsp.	sea salt
1 tsp.	white pepper
1/2	red pepper, diced

Method

1. Put the ginger, cinnamon stick, squash and sweet potato in a soup pot. Cover with vegetable stock. Bring to a boil; then reduce to a simmer.
2. While the vegetables are simmering in the soup pot, heat olive oil in a frying pan. Add onion and cook until caramelized, about 5 minutes.
3. Add white wine and chopped pears to the pan. Cook for 5 minutes until wine is reduced; then add to the soup pot.
4. When the squash and sweet potatoes are cooked, about 30 minutes, add the coconut milk, salt and pepper. Remove from heat. Take out the cinnamon stick.
5. Purée in a food processor or with a hand blender. To purée in a blender, first let the soup cool; then reheat to serve. With a hand blender, you can purée while the soup is still hot.
6. Garnish with finely diced red pepper and serve.

Caribbean Coconut and Red Pepper Soup

This unique crimson-coloured soup makes a wonderful first course for dinner. It's great for arousing the appetites of your guests.

Serves 6

Ingredients

2 1/2 tbsp.	sunflower oil
1	onion, peeled and sliced
3 cloves	garlic, minced
1	potato, peeled and diced
1 tbsp.	paprika
1/2 tsp.	chili powder
2 tbsp.	coriander, ground
1 tsp.	cayenne
1 tbsp.	tamari
2 cups	shredded cabbage
3 1/2 cups	canned crushed tomatoes
5 cups	Vegetable Stock (see p. 20)
1 tbsp.	raw sugar
1 or 2	hot red chilies, diced
2	red peppers, diced
1 cup	coconut milk
1 pinch	sea salt and black pepper

Method

1. Heat 2 tablespoons of sunflower oil over medium heat in the soup pot. Add the onion, garlic, potato, spices and tamari. Cook for 5 minutes until onion is soft.
2. Add the cabbage, tomatoes, vegetable stock, sugar and chilies. Simmer until potatoes are cooked.
3. In a separate pan, quickly sauté peppers at high heat in the remainder of the sunflower oil, until they are slightly charred but still crunchy.
4. Add the sautéed peppers to the soup pot along with the coconut milk, salt and pepper. Let simmer for 5 minutes.
5. Garnish with grated coconut or a slice of lemon and serve.

Carrot and Coriander Soup

I love this soup for its simplicity. Use organic carrots if you can, as they are sweeter and richer tasting.

Serves 6

Ingredients

2 tbsp.	canola oil
2	onions, peeled and chopped
3 tbsp.	coriander, ground
6 cloves	garlic, crushed
2 tbsp.	marjoram
3 large	carrots, peeled and chopped
1 medium	sweet potato, peeled and chopped
8 cups	Vegetable Stock (see p. 20)
1/2 cup	chopped fresh cilantro
1/2 tsp.	sea salt and cayenne pepper to taste

Method

1. Heat the canola oil over medium heat in a soup pot. Add the onions and cook until browned, about 5 minutes.
2. Add the coriander, garlic and marjoram to the browned onions and cook for 1 minute.
3. Add the carrots and sweet potato to the pot. Sauté for 1 minute.
4. Pour the vegetable stock into the pot of ingredients and bring to a boil. Let simmer until carrots and sweet potato are soft. Add the fresh cilantro, sea salt and cayenne pepper to taste.
5. Purée, using a hand blender or food processor. Garnish with a few sprigs of cilantro and serve.

Cuban Chick Pea and Potato Soup New!

This mildly spiced soup has a creamy texture from the chick peas and potato. It is hearty yet light at the same time. This soup tastes even better the day after it is made, once the flavours have had time to meld together. You can either cook the chick peas yourself or use canned, in which case just drain and rinse them before use.

Serves 6

Ingredients

3 tbsp.	olive oil
2	onions, peeled and chopped
4 stalks	celery, chopped
4 cloves	garlic, chopped
2	red bell peppers, diced
2 tsp.	cumin, ground
2 tsp.	fennel, ground
1/2 tsp.	dried thyme
1 tsp.	paprika
2 tsp.	sea salt
1 tsp.	black pepper, ground
1 pinch	cayenne pepper
8 cups	Vegetable Stock (see p. 20)
6	medium-sized white potatoes, peeled and chopped
4 cups	cooked chick peas
1 tbsp.	lemon juice
1 tbsp.	fresh parsley, chopped

Method

1. Heat olive oil over medium heat in a soup pot. Add onions, celery and garlic. Sauté until soft.
2. Add red peppers, cumin, fennel, thyme, paprika, sea salt, black pepper and cayenne.
3. Stir and sauté for a few seconds.
4. Add stock and potatoes. Bring to a boil; then reduce to a simmer and cook until potatoes are soft.
5. Add chick peas and lemon juice.
6. Bring back to a boil and then remove from heat.
7. Add parsley and stir.

Florentine Bean Soup (New!)

This soup is a big favourite of our staff and customers. It is rich, flavourful and very filling, perfect for those cold winter nights served with a big hunk of cornbread or multigrain pita. The white kidney beans should be soaked overnight in cold water to cut down on their cooking time. If you haven't had the time to soak them, you may need to add more stock. Or, to make it even easier, just use canned beans; add them with the spinach at the end of cooking. If you want to substitute a different kind of cooked greens, like kale or bok choy, add them a few minutes before the soup is ready to give them time to soften.

Serves 6

Ingredients

2 tbsp.	olive oil
1	onion, peeled and chopped
3 cloves	garlic, chopped
1 stalk	celery, chopped
1	carrot, peeled and chopped
1/2 tsp.	dried thyme
1/2 tsp.	dried sage
1 pinch	dried rosemary
1 pinch	cayenne pepper
1 tsp.	garlic powder
1/2 tsp.	ground white pepper
1/3 cup	dry red lentils
1/3 cup	dry green lentils
1/3 cup	dry green split peas
1/3 cup	pearl barley
1 cup	dry white kidney beans (soaked overnight)
1/4 cup	chopped fresh curly parsley
12 cups	Vegetable Stock (see p. 20)
8 cups	spinach, chopped and loosely packed
	sea salt to taste

Method

1. Heat olive oil over medium heat in a soup pot. Add the onion, garlic, celery and carrots. Sauté until soft.
2. Add the thyme, sage, rosemary, cayenne, garlic powder and white pepper, and stir.
3. Add the lentils, split peas, barley, beans, parsley and stock.

4. Bring to a boil; then reduce to a simmer and cook until the white beans are tender.
5. Remove from heat.
6. Add spinach, stir and add salt to taste.

Green Split Pea Soup

This is a classic country split pea recipe without the smoked ham. The soup gradually thickens as it cools. For reheating, just add enough water or stock to get the desired consistency.

Serves 6

Ingredients

2 tbsp.	sunflower oil
1	onion, peeled and diced
1	carrot, peeled and diced
1 stalk	celery, diced
1/2 inch	ginger root, peeled and minced
8 cups	Vegetable Stock (see p. 20)
1 1/2 cups	dry green split peas
1	potato, peeled and diced
1 tsp.	powdered rosemary
1	bay leaf
1 pinch	cayenne
1/2 tsp.	sea salt
1/2 tsp.	white pepper
1 tsp.	tamari
1/2 tsp.	apple cider vinegar

Method

1. In a soup pot, heat the sunflower oil over medium heat. Add the onion, carrot, celery and ginger. Sauté until the onions are soft.
2. Add the vegetable stock and green split peas. Bring to a boil; then reduce to a simmer. Cook for 1/2 hour, or until peas are almost cooked.
3. Add potato and remaining ingredients. Cook for another 15 minutes.
4. Remove bay leaf and garnish with a sprig of rosemary or a slice of lemon.

Marrakesh Curried Stew

My father was born in Marrakesh and my mother was born in Casablanca, Morocco. This is one of my original recipes, borrowed from my mother. I first prepared it at my little counter at the Queen Street Market. This stew is delicious on its own, on a plate of couscous or over a bowl of rice. You can also try it with a drizzle of Tahini Sauce (see page 98).

Serves 6

Ingredients

2	onions, peeled and cut in chunks
2	carrots, peeled and cut in chunks
2 cups	Vegetable Stock (see p. 20)
2 cups	coconut milk
1 tsp.	cinnamon
1/2 tsp.	cayenne pepper
2 tbsp.	curry powder
4 tbsp.	cumin, ground
1/2 tsp.	turmeric
2	white potatoes, cut in chunks
1	sweet potato, cut in chunks
1 small	eggplant, cut in chunks
6 cloves	garlic, minced
2	green peppers, cut in chunks
1	red pepper, cut in chunks
1	zucchini, cut in chunks
2 cups	cooked or canned chick peas
3 tbsp.	raisins
2 tbsp.	grated coconut
	sea salt to taste

Method

1. Put the onions and carrots in a large pot with 1/2 cup of vegetable stock and cook over medium heat until onion softens a bit, about 3 minutes.
2. Add the coconut milk and the spices. Cook for 1 minute, while stirring.

3. Add the white and sweet potatoes and the rest of the stock. Cover and let cook for 5 minutes.
4. Add the remaining ingredients. Stir, cover and cook until vegetables are just soft, about 20 minutes.
5. To bring out all the flavours, season to taste with a pinch or two of sea salt.

Nepalese Dal

In India and Nepal this soup is traditionally served, thick as stew, over a bowl of steamed basmati rice. The dal will thicken once it cools down. Toast the grated coconut for a couple of minutes to enhance its flavour and sweetness.

Serves 6

Ingredients

3/4 cup	dry yellow split peas
3/4 cup	dry green split peas
10 cups	Vegetable Stock (see p. 20)
1	carrot, peeled and chopped
2 tbsp.	sunflower oil
2 tsp.	mustard seeds
1 tbsp.	cumin, ground
2 tsp.	coriander, ground
1 tsp.	crushed chilies
1 tsp.	turmeric
1	potato, peeled and chopped
1 tbsp.	grated coconut
1 tsp.	tamari
1 small	red pepper, chopped
3/4 cup	frozen green peas
	sea salt, to taste

Method

1. Put the split peas in a soup pot with the vegetable stock. Bring to a boil and reduce to a simmer. When the split peas are half-cooked, about 15 minutes, add the carrot.

2. In a saucepan, heat the sunflower oil over medium heat. Drop the mustard seeds into the pan. When the mustard seeds start to pop, turn off the heat and add the cumin, coriander, chili, turmeric and potato. Mix well together and let sit for 5 minutes.
3. Add the spices, potato and grated coconut to the soup pot. When the split peas and potato are soft, add the tamari, red pepper and green peas. Season to taste with sea salt.
4. Garnish with cilantro and serve.

Red Bean and Lager Chili

The lager is the secret ingredient that gives this popular stew its robust flavour. A microbrewed lager beer with no preservatives is the best way to go with this recipe. This is great served with a dollop of Tofu Sour Cream (see page 107).

Serves 6

Ingredients

1 tbsp.	cumin, ground
1/4 cup	olive oil
2	onions, peeled and diced
5 cloves	garlic, minced
1/2 stalk	celery, chopped
1	hot banana chili, minced
1	green pepper, chopped
2 tbsp.	chili powder
2 tbsp.	cocoa powder
1 2-inch	cinnamon stick
6 cups	crushed tomatoes
2 cups	red kidney beans, cooked
1	carrot, peeled and chopped
1	zucchini, chopped
1	red pepper, chopped
12 oz.	microbrewed lager beer
1 cup	cilantro, chopped
	sea salt, to taste

Method

1. Toast the ground cumin in a dry, hot pan to release the flavour. Set aside.
2. In a soup pot, sauté the onions, garlic, celery, banana chili and green pepper in oil until soft.
3. Stir in the cumin, chili powder, cocoa and cinnamon stick.
4. Add the remaining ingredients, except the cilantro, and bring to a boil. Reduce heat to low and let chili simmer until all vegetables are tender.
5. Remove from heat. Remove cinnamon stick; add cilantro and sea salt to taste.

Spicy Tomato with Chipotle and Spinach Soup

To roast a red pepper, put it directly onto a gas flame or an electric burner and keep turning it until the skin has blackened or lifted away from the flesh. Put into a bowl, cover with plastic wrap and let sit until cooled. Then just peel it, remove the seeds and it is ready to go.

Serves 6

Ingredients

2 tbsp.	olive oil
1	onion, peeled and chopped
3 cloves	garlic, minced
1	carrot, peeled and chopped
1 stalk	celery, chopped
4	medium-sized tomatoes, chopped
1	roasted red pepper, peeled, seeded and chopped
2	chipotle peppers, chopped
1 tbsp.	adobo sauce (from the can of chipotles)
3 cups	canned crushed tomatoes
3 cups	Vegetable Stock (see p. 20)
1 tsp.	sea salt
4 cups	spinach, chopped

Method

1. Heat oil over medium heat in soup pot. Add onion, garlic, carrot and celery. Sauté until slightly browned.
2. Add chopped tomatoes, roasted red pepper, chipotles, adobo sauce, crushed tomatoes and stock. Bring to a boil and cook until carrots are soft.
3. Remove from heat and purée.
4. Add salt and spinach. Stir and serve.

Sweet Potato and Coconut Soup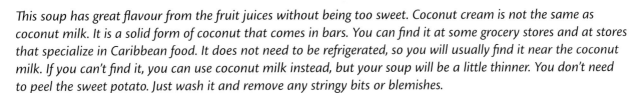

This soup has great flavour from the fruit juices without being too sweet. Coconut cream is not the same as coconut milk. It is a solid form of coconut that comes in bars. You can find it at some grocery stores and at stores that specialize in Caribbean food. It does not need to be refrigerated, so you will usually find it near the coconut milk. If you can't find it, you can use coconut milk instead, but your soup will be a little thinner. You don't need to peel the sweet potato. Just wash it and remove any stringy bits or blemishes.

Serves 6

Ingredients

2 tbsp.	olive oil
2	onions, peeled and chopped
2 stalks	celery, chopped
2 tbsp.	ginger, peeled and finely minced
1 1/2 tsp.	curry powder
1/4 tsp.	nutmeg
1/4 tsp.	sea salt
5 cups	Vegetable Stock (see p. 20)
5 cups	chopped sweet potato
1/4 cup	lemon juice
3/4 cup	unsweetened pineapple juice
3/4 cup	unsweetened orange juice
1 bar	coconut cream, chopped

Method

1. Heat olive oil over medium heat in a soup pot. Add onion, celery and ginger. Sauté until soft.
2. Add curry powder and nutmeg to onion mixture. Stir and cook for a few seconds.
3. Add salt, stock and sweet potatoes. Bring to a boil; then reduce to a simmer and cook until sweet potatoes are soft.
4. Add remaining ingredients and cook until coconut bar has dissolved.
5. Remove from heat and purée until smooth.
6. Add salt and pepper to taste. Add more stock, if necessary, to achieve desired consistency.

Tuscan White Bean with Pesto Soup New!

This soup is reminiscent of Florence and other parts of Tuscany where they serve delicious white beans as a side dish. It is very quick to make. You can either add the pesto directly to the soup and stir it in, or serve it as a garnish for the soup. If you have a squeeze bottle, you can put a swirl on top of the soup or just spoon a dollop into the middle and let your guests stir it in themselves. By blending half of the soup, you get a creamy texture without adding any dairy ingredients.

Serves 6

Ingredients

1 tbsp.	olive oil
1	onion, peeled and chopped
3 cloves	garlic, minced
1 cup	white wine
2 tsp.	dried basil
1 tsp.	dried tarragon
3	tomatoes, chopped
2 19-oz. cans	white kidney beans, drained and rinsed
4 cups	Vegetable Stock (see p. 20)
1 tsp.	sea salt
6 tsp.	Spinach Basil Pesto (see p. 105)

Method

1. Heat oil over medium heat in a soup pot. Add onion and garlic. Sauté until onions are soft.
2. Add wine, basil and tarragon. Bring to a boil and let simmer until wine is reduced by half.
3. Add tomatoes, beans, stock and salt. Bring back to a boil; then reduce heat and let simmer until tomatoes are very soft. This should only take a few minutes once the soup is boiling.
4. Remove from heat.
5. Put half of the soup into a separate container and purée it with a hand blender until completely smooth. (If you are using a regular blender, let the soup cool before blending; then reheat.)
6. Add the purée and the pesto into the rest of the soup, stir and serve.

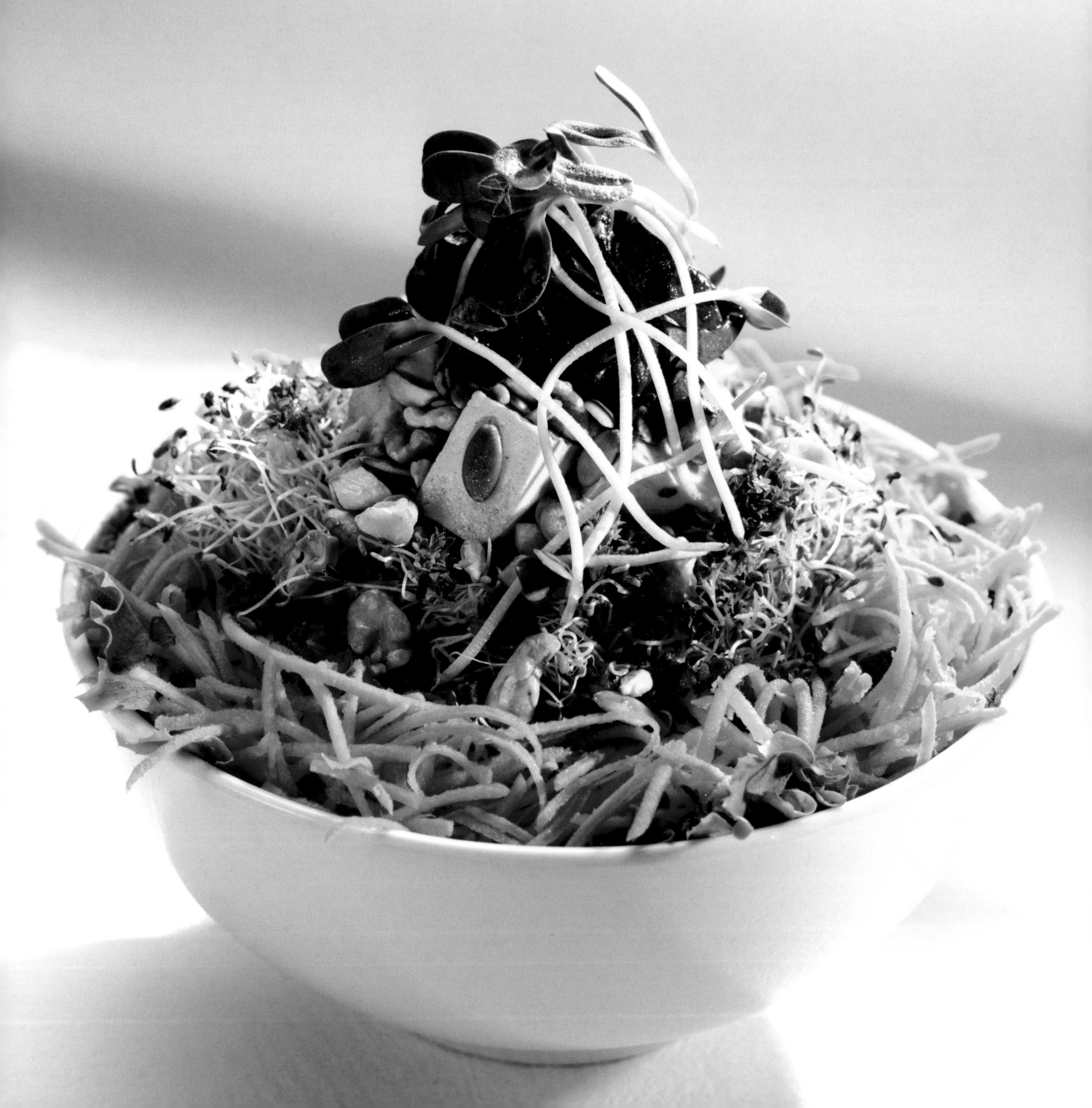

Salads

Life sustains life; when the fibre-rich fruits and vegetables we eat are raw, uncooked and unprocessed, we get high-energy fuel loaded with vitamins, minerals and live enzymes for the nourishment of our cells, tissues, glands, organs and every part of our bodies. A diet consisting of only processed, cooked or fried foods is one which creates more work for the body's waste management system and drains the body of precious energy, leaving you feeling sluggish and tired. Salads and raw foods fill you up without dragging you down. They digest easily and are naturally high in distilled water, which helps the organs do their job of flushing out toxins. Like a broom, raw fibre sweeps the build-up of waste from the intestines and helps keep a clean house.

Here are seven lovely salads guaranteed to satisfy your earthly needs. You can pick your own favourite lettuces for these salads. At Fresh we like to use a spring mix or baby spinach for our salads. Find a salad dressing (see page 79) you really like to make your salad as delicious and enjoyable as possible.

California Classic Salad (New!)

This deeply satisfying salad is highly popular amongst my beautiful girlfriends Kim, Debra, Pheona and Anita, and our women customers in general. The ingredients in this salad go so well together every bite is a pleasant taste sensation of flavour and textures. Heart of palm is a vegetable harvested from the inner core and growing bud of certain palm trees. Given that harvesting is a costly and labour-intensive task, palm hearts are regarded as a delicacy. Hearts of palm are available canned at specialty food and grocery stores. I recommend topping this salad with Marinated Tofu Cubes (see page 90) or Crispy Tofu Coating (see page 87) for added protein.

Serves 2

Ingredients

8 cups	spring mix lettuce
1/2 cup	cooked white kidney beans
2 tbsp.	Spinach Basil Pesto (see p. 105)
1	avocado, sliced
1/2 cup	hearts of palm, sliced
1/4 cup	toasted pecans
10	grape tomatoes

Method

1. In a small bowl, mix white kidney beans with pesto.
2. Toss lettuce in dressing of your choice and place in large bowls.
3. Top with remaining ingredients and serve.

Mega Life Salad

This main course salad is highly satisfying and filling. That's why it has been one of our top sellers for the past 12 years. It's the steamed spinach and marinated tofu that clinch it for me.

Serves 1

Ingredients

4 cups	mixed lettuce greens
1	carrot, peeled and grated
1/4 cup	grated beets
1/2 pack	alfalfa sprouts
6 cubes	Marinated Tofu (see p. 90)
2 tbsp.	chopped parsley
3 tbsp.	Toasted Nuts and Seeds (see p. 4)
1 cup	spinach, steamed
1/2 cup	sunflower sprouts

Method

1. Toss lettuce with your choice of dressing (see p. 79) and place in large bowl.
2. Make a ring of grated carrot around the edge of the bowl. On top of the lettuce, in the centre of the ring, put some grated beets. On top of the grated beets, form a doughnut shape out of the alfalfa sprouts. In the centre of the doughnut, put tofu cubes, parsley, nuts and seeds.
3. Arrange steamed spinach in a pile on top of the nuts and seeds. Drizzle with 1 tablespoon dressing.
4. Garnish with sunflower sprouts and serve.

Quick Protein Salad (New!)

Formerly known as the Mega Protein Salad, one of our originals, we recently jazzed up this well-loved salad with grape tomatoes, currants and baby spinach leaves. The chickpeas, sunflower seeds and grilled tempeh provide an excellent, easily digestible source of protein.

Serves 2

Ingredients

4 slices	Marinated Tempeh (see p. 89)
1 cup	cooked chick peas
8 cups	baby spinach
1 pack	alfalfa sprouts
1/4 cup	toasted sunflower seeds
10	grape tomatoes
4 tbsp.	currants
1/4	cucumber, diced

Method

1. Grill or broil the Marinated Tempeh slices in the oven until brown on both sides, about 5 minutes.
2. Toss baby spinach in dressing of your choice and place in large bowls.
3. Form a doughnut shape out of the alfalfa sprouts and place in middle of salad. In centre of alfalfa, put the chick peas and then the sunflower seeds.
4. Arrange diced cucumber, grape tomatoes and currants around edge of salad.
5. Place tempeh on top and drizzle with your choice of dressing (see p. 79). Serve.

Mega Caesar Salad

This salad is so filling that I can usually eat only half. Often I roll up the other half in a tortilla for lunch the next day.

Serves 1

Ingredients

4 cups	torn romaine lettuce
1/4 cup	croutons
1 serving	Creamy Caesar Dressing (see p. 82)
1 cup	grated carrot
1/2 pack	alfalfa sprouts
6 cubes	Marinated Tofu (see p. 90)
2 tbsp.	sunflower seeds, toasted
6	cucumber slices
6	green pepper slices
6	Kalamata olives

Method

1. Toss romaine lettuce and croutons in Creamy Caesar Dressing and place in a large salad bowl.
2. Arrange grated carrot around the edge of the bowl and form a ring of alfalfa sprouts in the centre. Place tofu cubes in the middle. Sprinkle sunflower seeds on the tofu cubes.
3. Arrange the cucumber, green pepper and olives around the top of the salad. Garnish with a wedge of lemon and serve.

Parisian Salad (New!)

This salad is the Fresh version of a Salade Nicoise. For added protein and extra flavour, top it off with Crispy Tofu cubes (see page 87). Our House Dressing (see page 80) pairs nicely with this salad.

Serves 2

Ingredients

2 cups	sugar snap peas
6	mini red potatoes
2 cloves	garlic, minced
1 tsp.	dried dill
3 tbsp.	olive oil
1/4 tsp.	sea salt
8 cups	baby spinach
10	Kalamata olives
10	grape tomatoes
2 tbsp.	red onion, finely diced
2 tsp.	sesame seeds

Method

To Prepare Sugar Snap Peas
1. Bring a small pot of water to a boil and add the peas. Let them cook for about 1 minute, or until they look bright green and are just starting to get tender.
2. Drain and rinse under cold water until no heat remains.

To Prepare Potatoes
1. Bring a small pot of water to a boil.
2. Cut each potato into halves or quarters, depending on how big they are. They should be around the same size once cut so that they will cook at the same rate. Add potatoes to boiling water and cook until tender. Drain and let cool slightly.
3. Put potatoes into a bowl and toss with olive oil, salt, garlic and dill.
4. Heat frying pan over medium heat and add potatoes. Cook for a few minutes, turning them individually to make sure all sides get browned. Remove from heat and let cool.

To Assemble Salad
1. Toss baby spinach with dressing of your choice and place in large bowls.
2. Place potatoes and peas in the middle with the tomatoes and olives around the edge. Sprinkle with the red onion and sesame seeds, and serve.

Portobello and Walnut Salad

Try a serving of Marinated Tofu Steaks (see page 90) with this warm salad, for a little extra protein and texture.

Serves 2

Ingredients

2 tbsp.	olive oil
4	portobello mushrooms, sliced
2 tbsp.	balsamic vinegar
8 cups	mixed lettuce greens
1/2 cup	chopped walnuts

Method

1. Heat oil in frying pan over high heat. Add sliced mushrooms and balsamic vinegar. Let them cook fully on one side; then turn them over to get a nice brown colour and caramelized effect.
2. While mushrooms cook, toss lettuce with your choice of dressing (see p. 79). Divide lettuce and pile it onto two dinner plates.
3. When the mushrooms are almost ready, add the walnuts and toss. Leave on heat just long enough to warm the walnuts through. If you cook them too long, the walnuts will develop a bitter taste.
4. Divide mushrooms and walnuts on top of each plate of salad greens and serve.

Big Sur Salad

As a teenager, I had the privilege of visiting the Esalen Institute in Big Sur, California. It was there that I ate my first real vegetarian meal. This salad reminds me of my time there. Don't worry if you can't find these exact sprouts. You can use any type of sprout you find tasty, including alfalfa, broccoli or pea sprouts.

Serves 2

Ingredients

1	red pepper
8 cups	mixed lettuce greens
1/2	cucumber, sliced
2 cups	sunflower sprouts
8	marinated sundried tomatoes (see p. 106)
2 cups	buckwheat sprouts

Method

1. Cut red pepper in half vertically. Remove seeds and grill or broil the flesh until just starting to blacken. Remove from heat and slice each half into six.
2. Toss the salad greens with your choice of dressing (see p. 79) and place in two large salad bowls. Arrange red peppers and cucumber slices around the edge of each bowl.
3. In the centre of each salad, place a pile of sunflower sprouts. Top with sundried tomatoes and buckwheat sprouts. Drizzle with 1 teaspoon of dressing and serve.

Sandwiches and Wraps

Wraps are all the rage these days and it's not hard to understand why. For people on the go a wrap is a quick and convenient way to eat a healthy meal while walking, driving or even riding your bicycle without spilling anything on yourself. A tortilla wrap fills you up on the ingredients inside, not on the bread.

The nori roll, a Japanese creation, has crossed over to North America to become a popular way to eat a breadless sandwich with many different fillings. Toasted nori is the most easily digested of the seaweeds and also a rich source of protein and vitamins B and A. Still, nothing beats a good sandwich on home-baked bread with the right spread and fresh ingredients.

Holiday Wrap New!

A new addition to our menu this year, this wrap is delicious, quick and easy to make.

Serves 4

Ingredients

4	12-inch whole wheat tortillas
1 batch	House Mayo (see p. 103)
1	avocado, sliced
1 batch	Marinated Tofu Cubes (see p. 90)
1 pack	alfalfa sprouts
2	tomatoes, diced
1/2	English cucumber, diced
1/4	red onion, peeled and diced
2 cups	lettuce
2 cups	grated carrot

Method

1. Heat tortillas on a grill or in the oven.
2. Top with a quarter of the remaining ingredients; then fold in edges and roll up.
3. Repeat for each serving.

Nori Roll

This roll-up is great to take to work for lunch or to eat later since it keeps well unrefrigerated and won't get soggy.

Serves 4

Ingredients

4 sheets	toasted nori
4 cups	sweet brown rice, cooked (see p. 4)
2 cups	grated carrot
2	avocados, sliced

1 pack	alfalfa sprouts
1	red pepper, sliced
	tamari or soy sauce for dipping

Method

1. Fill a small bowl with warm water. Use this water for wetting your fingers in the following steps. You can also use this water to moisten the ends of the nori so they stick together when you roll it up in step 4.
2. Lay a sheet of nori on a flat surface. Wet your fingers and spread a quarter of the rice onto the nori, leaving about an inch uncovered at the top of the sheet.
3. Place a portion of the grated carrot, avocado slices, alfalfa and red pepper horizontally about half way down the rice.
4. Wet your fingers again and roll the nori into a thick cigar shape.
5. Use a sharp, wet knife to cut the Nori Roll diagonally in half.
6. Serve with tamari or soy sauce for dipping. Repeat for each serving.

Kathmandu Wrap

This tasty curry-flavoured wrap is warm and very filling. It makes a nice lunch for two along with a side salad each.

Serves 4

Ingredients

4	12-inch whole wheat tortillas
1 batch	Curried Garbanzo Filling (see p. 101), heated
1 pack	alfalfa sprouts
2	tomatoes, sliced
1/2	cucumber, sliced
1 batch	Tahini Sauce (see p. 98)

Method

1. Heat tortillas on a grill or in the oven.
2. Spread a thick layer of warm Curried Garbanzo Filling down the centre of one tortilla.
3. Top with alfalfa, tomato and cucumber.
4. Roll the tortilla, tucking in the two ends as you go.
5. Serve a small bowl of Tahini Sauce on the side for dipping. Repeat for each serving.

Black Bean Burrito

For extra protein, flavour and texture, add two slices of grilled Marinated Tempeh (see page 89) and Tofu Sour Cream (see page 107).

Serves 4

Ingredients

4	12-inch whole wheat tortillas
2	tomatoes, diced
1 bunch	cilantro, chopped
1/2	cucumber, chopped
1/2	red onion, peeled and chopped
2 cups	shredded lettuce
1 batch	Black Bean Filling (see p. 100), heated
2	avocados, sliced

Method

1. Heat tortillas on a grill or in the oven.
2. Toss the diced tomato, cilantro, cucumber, red onion and lettuce together in a small mixing bowl.
3. Spread a thick layer of warm Black Bean Filling across the centre of one tortilla. Spoon on a portion of the tomato mixture. Top with avocado slices.
4. Roll the tortilla, tucking in the two ends as you go. Repeat for each serving.

Roti for Life

The roti is a popular and healthy fast food in the West Indies. There are many types of fillings, including a wide range of choice for vegetarians. A great deal of pride is taken in the taste of the roti, with each shop making its own version from scratch. There are three steps to this recipe: preparing the filling, making the roti shell and wrapping the roti.

Serves 6

Ingredients

Roti Filling

1 batch	Marrakesh Curried Stew (see p. 29), heated

Roti Shell

2 cups	white flour, unbleached
1/4 tsp.	baking soda
1/2 tsp.	sea salt
1 tsp.	whole cumin seed, toasted
1/4 tsp.	curry powder
2/3 cup	plain soymilk
2 tbsp.	sunflower oil

Method

Prepare the Marrakesh Curried Stew and leave on the stove at low heat while making the roti shells.

Making the Roti Shell

The roti shell can be used to wrap any hot stew or filling of your choice or as a side of tasty warm bread to accompany a bowl of hearty soup and salad. The dough can be stored in the refrigerator for up to a week.

1. In a large mixing bowl, combine all dry ingredients.
2. Combine the wet ingredients separately; then pour into the centre of the dry ingredients. Gradually mix to form a ball of dough.
3. Knead gently for 1 minute on a floured surface. Use the heel of your hand to push the dough away from you; then pull it back with your fingers. Repeat this motion until the dough feels smooth.
4. Put the dough in a lightly oiled bowl and cover with plastic wrap. Let it sit for at least half an hour.
5. Divide the dough into 6 equal portions and form into balls.
6. On a lightly floured surface, roll out each ball with a rolling pin. Each circle should be about the size of a dinner plate and fairly thin.
7. Fry in a dry pan or skillet over medium heat for about 2 minutes on each side or until lightly browned. Repeat for each serving.

Wrapping the Roti

Put the cooked roti shell on a small plate. Ladle one 8-ounce serving of warm Marrakesh Curried Stew onto centre of the roti shell. Fold all sides in to form a square. Place a large dinner plate over the roti, face down. Pick up both plates and in one motion flip them over. The roti should now be on the large plate, right side up. Serve hot with a side of steamed brown rice or a garden salad. Repeat for each serving.

Urban Cowboy Sandwich

This is a triple-decker sandwich for the vegetarian cowboy or cowgirl.

Serves 4

Ingredients

1 batch	Marinated Tempeh (see p. 89)
12 slices	multigrain bread
1 batch	House Mayo (see p. 103)
1 pack	alfalfa sprouts
2	tomatoes, sliced
1	red onion, sliced
6	lettuce leaves

Method

1. Grill or broil the tempeh.
2. Toast 3 slices of bread. Spread each slice of toast with a thin layer of House Mayo.
3. On one slice of bread put alfalfa sprouts, tomato and onion. Lay on a second slice of bread and place a leaf of lettuce and three slices of tempeh on top. Top with the last slice of bread, press down and cut in half diagonally.

Magic Tofu Wrap (New!)

The Crispy Tofu Coating is so popular we are always searching for new ways to offer it. This wrap is loved by kids especially; it's a great way to get them to eat their tofu.

Serves 4

Ingredients

4	12-inch whole wheat tortillas
1 batch	House Mayo (see p. 103)
1 batch	Crispy Tofu Coating (see p. 87)
1 batch	Marinated Tofu Steaks (see p. 90)
1 pack	alfalfa sprouts
2 cups	grated carrot
2 cups	lettuce
1/4	red onion
2	tomatoes, diced
1/2	English cucumber, diced
4 tbsp.	olive oil

Method

1. Heat olive oil in frying pan over medium heat.
2. Dredge Tofu Steaks in Crispy Tofu Coating and cook in pan until browned on both sides. Set aside.
3. Heat tortillas on a grill or in the oven.
4. Top with a quarter of the ingredients; then fold in edges and roll up.
5. Repeat for each serving.

Fez Pita

This sandwich is great, especially if the pita is a thick whole grain and very fresh. Authentic Middle Eastern grocery stores usually have the best handmade pitas and fresh prepared hummus.

Serves 4

Ingredients

1	eggplant, sliced
1	zucchini, sliced
4	pitas
1 batch	Hummus (see p. 104)
1 batch	Sundried Tomato Paste (see p. 106)

Method

1. Brush the eggplant and zucchini with olive oil to avoid sticking. Grill or broil the slices in the oven until tender.
2. Heat pitas on a grill or in the oven.
3. Cut off the top 1/8 of the pita. Spread a thick layer of Hummus on one side inside the pita. Spread the Sundried Tomato Paste on the other.
4. Stuff the pita with grilled eggplant and zucchini. Repeat for each serving.

Veggie Burgers

I have searched high, low and all around the country for the ultimate veggie burger. Most are too dry, some have no flavour, others are excessively spiced to taste like hamburger meat and almost all of them fall apart in your hands. Often veggie burgers have hidden ingredients such as eggs or dairy products holding the patty together and are cooked on the grill with meats. This is a real turn-off for me and seems to defeat the whole purpose of having a veggie burger on the menu in the first place.

At Fresh we take our burgers very seriously. They are mouthwateringly good in their own right and no poor substitute for real meat. Our high-protein burgers are made with a variety of vegetables, grains, tofu, nuts, seeds, herbs and spices. The Fresh Burger is the patty we use for all our burgers on the menu. We then add different sauces, toppings and garnishes to create new burger choices, which are grilled and served on a toasted whole wheat kaiser bun. Since we pile our burgers high, the bun should be soft so you can get your mouth around it.

Fresh Burger Mix

These burger patties are so delicious and filling they can be served without the bun. The burger mix keeps for up to three days in the fridge and can be safely frozen.

Makes 6 burger patties

Ingredients

1 cup	filtered water
1/2 cup	uncooked hulled millet
1/2 cup	uncooked pearl barley
3 tbsp.	sunflower seeds
1 1/2 tbsp.	chopped almonds
1 clove	garlic, chopped
2 tbsp.	chopped parsley
1/2	red onion, peeled and chopped
1/4 cup	grated carrot
3/4 cup	firm tofu, chopped
3 tbsp.	grated beets
1 1/2 tbsp.	tamari
2 tbsp.	spelt flour
2 tbsp.	Engevita (inactive) yeast
1/4 tsp.	cayenne
1/4 tsp.	chili powder
1 tsp.	curry powder
1 tsp.	sea salt
1 tsp.	cornstarch
3 tbsp.	mixed herbs
2 tbsp.	carrot juice or water (if needed)

Method

1. Put the millet, barley and 1 cup of water in a small pot over high heat and stir. Bring to a boil, then reduce heat and let cook until the water is absorbed. Put the grains in a large mixing bowl. Let cool.
2. While the grains are cooking, grind the seeds and nuts in a food processor. Add these to the ingredients in the mixing bowl.

3. In the same food processor, purée the garlic, parsley, onion and carrot. When they are chopped fine, add the tofu and process until smooth.
4. Put this mixture in the mixing bowl with the nuts, seeds and grains.
   Add the remaining ingredients—except the carrot juice—and mix thoroughly with a large spoon. Add the carrot juice or water if the mix is too dry for shaping into patties.
5. Divide and form into 6 patties.
6. Fry, broil or grill the burgers until slightly crisp and brown on both sides, about 5 minutes each side.

Life Burger

Top the Fresh Burger patty (see page 58) with Herb Tofu Mayo (see page 102), alfalfa sprouts, red onion, sliced tomato and a leaf of lettuce.

Miso Burger

Top the Fresh Burger patty (see page 58) with heated Miso Gravy (see page 91), grilled sliced tomato, chopped green onion and a leaf of lettuce.

Thai Burger

Top the Fresh Burger patty (see page 58) with heated Thai Peanut Sauce (see page 97), fresh cilantro, chopped green onion, crisp bean sprouts, lettuce and tomato.

Mushroom Onion Burger

Top the Fresh Burger patty (see page 58) with sautéed button or portobello mushrooms and onions. Garnish with tomato and lettuce.

Bunless Burger (New!)

Top the Fresh Burger patty (see page 58) with grilled eggplant and red pepper, House Mayo (see page 103), alfalfa sprouts, red onion and cucumber. Garnish with tomato and lettuce.

Rice Bowls

At Fresh, we serve steamed brown basmati rice in our rice bowls. Basmati rice, originally farmed in India, is an aromatic long grain with a nutty flavour. Brown rice is nutritionally superior to white rice. When the shell of the rice grain is removed to process a polished white rice, the bran, fibre, germ, essential oils and other nutrients are also removed. Whole brown rice is a rich source of B vitamins and complex carbohydrates. The B vitamins revive the exhausted nervous system from the effects of stress and high activity, while the complex carbs provide a gradual release of fuel for your body.

In many cultures, rice symbolizes the creation of life and fertility. This is where the custom of throwing rice at a bride and groom came from. In any case, rice is the world's most highly consumed food. At the restaurants, we offer our rice bowls on soba noodles for a delicious alternative. I would recommend a deep Japanese-style ceramic bowl for best results in presentation. A traditional rice bowl will also make eating with chopsticks much easier.

Simple Rice Bowl

The Simple Rice Bowl holds a special place on our menu for those who crave a comforting bowl of brown rice. Added flavour and creaminess is provided by the combination of tahini and tamari sauce. This is also a good starting point from which to build an entire meal in a bowl. At Fresh, we offer this rice bowl topped with Marinated Tofu Cubes (see page 90) or Marinated Tempeh (see page 89). Kids love this one, too.

Serves 4

Ingredients

4 cups	cooked brown basmati rice (see p. 3)
1 batch	Tahini Sauce (see p. 98)
8 tsp.	tamari
2	carrots, grated
1 bunch	parsley, chopped
1	lemon, cut in wedges

Method

1. Put 1 cup of brown basmati rice in a medium rice bowl.
2. Drizzle 2 tablespoons of Tahini Sauce and 2 teaspoons of tamari on the rice.
3. Garnish with grated carrots, chopped parsley and a wedge of lemon. Repeat for each serving.

Buddha Rice Bowl

The Buddha is our most popular rice bowl, by far, for newcomers to Fresh. I remember creating this protein-rich rice bowl over 16 years ago at my tiny lunch counter in the Queen Street Market. It was a hit from the start. That was when I realized that, as a general rule, people will order anything with peanut sauce because it's familiar to them. The good news is that our Thai Peanut Sauce is wonderfully natural, simple and healthy, with no added oils or sweeteners.

Serves 4

Ingredients

6 cups	cooked brown basmati rice (see p. 3)
1 1/2 cups	Marinated Tofu Cubes (see p. 90)
1 batch	Thai Peanut Sauce, heated (see p. 97)
4 cups	bean sprouts
1 bunch	cilantro, chopped
1/2	cucumber, sliced and cut into half-moon shapes
1	tomato, sliced and cut into half-moon shapes
1	lemon, cut in wedges

Method

1. Put 1 1/2 cups of cooked brown basmati rice in a large rice bowl.
2. Top with a portion of Marinated Tofu Cubes in the middle.
3. Pour one 6-ounce ladle of warm Thai Peanut Sauce over the tofu and rice. Be sure to cover all the tofu with sauce to warm it up.
4. Put a handful of bean sprouts on top of the sauce, piling as high as possible. On top of the bean sprouts, place a few leaves of cilantro—or more if you love cilantro like I do.
5. Around the edge of the bowl, arrange four slices of cucumber and tomato.
6. Garnish with a wedge of lemon. Repeat for each serving.

Energy Rice Bowl (New!)

I think we can agree that energy is something we all want more of. This high-carb rice bowl gives you the fuel you need in order to have more energy throughout your day or night. Although it may take a little extra work to make the Coconut Curry Sauce and Curried Garbanzo Filling, it's worth it. If you have some leftover, you can also use these two sauces to prepare the Indian Dosas (see page 11) or the Kathmandu Wrap (see page 49).

Serves 4

Ingredients

6 cups	cooked brown basmati rice (see p. 3)
1 batch	Coconut Curry Sauce (see p. 86)
1 batch	Curried Garbanzo Filling (see p. 101)
1 1/2 cups	Marinated Tofu Cubes (see p. 90)
2	tomatoes, diced
1/2	small red onion, peeled and diced
1/2	English cucumber, diced
2 cups	sunflower sprouts
1 batch	Tahini Sauce (see p. 98)

Method

1. Put 1 1/2 cups of cooked brown basmati rice in a large rice bowl.
2. Top with Coconut Curry Sauce, Garbanzo Filling, Tofu Cubes, tomatoes, red onion and cucumber.
3. Place sunflower sprouts in a nice high pile and drizzle with Tahini Sauce. Repeat for each serving.

Ninja Rice Bowl (New!)

Oh, the Ninja! We all love this rice bowl at Fresh. The combination of brown rice and salad greens strikes the perfect balance and makes for a very satisfying but not too filling meal-in-a-bowl. One of the reasons our customers love this rice bowl is the Crispy Tofu cubes on top. I love the Wasabi Dill Dressing, which can double as a dressing for your other salads at home.

Serves 2

Ingredients

16	**Marinated Tofu Cubes (see p. 90)**
1 batch	**Crispy Tofu Coating (see p. 87)**
3 tbsp.	**olive oil**
2 cups	**cooked brown basmati rice (see p. 3)**
1 1/2 cups	**Wasabi Dill Dressing (see p. 81)**
8 cups	**mixed lettuce greens**
6	**marinated sundried tomatoes (see p. 106)**
1 cup	**sunflower sprouts**
2 tbsp.	**Ninja 2 Sauce (see p. 92)**

Method

1. Toss Marinated Tofu Cubes in Crispy Tofu Coating. Heat olive oil in pan over medium heat, add tofu cubes and cook until browned on all sides.
2. Put 1 cup cooked brown basmati rice in large rice bowl and drizzle with a portion of Wasabi Dill Dressing.
3. Toss lettuce with Wasabi Dill Dressing and pile on top of rice.
4. Arrange marinated sundried tomatoes on top of lettuce.
5. Drizzle Ninja 2 Sauce on top of lettuce.
6. Make a little nest with the sunflower sprouts in the centre and put Crispy Tofu cubes in the nest.
7. Repeat for each serving.

Dragon Rice Bowl

Each one of our rice bowls has a special "something" that makes it stand out and beckon your name even before you realize you're hungry. The Buddha has the Thai Peanut Sauce, the Ninja has the Crispy Tofu cubes and the Dragon has the rich and savoury Miso Gravy. This intensely flavoured gravy has a loyal following that goes back to the early days in the Queen Street Market when Fresh was called Juice for Life.

Serves 4

Ingredients

1 large	zucchini, sliced diagonally
3	tomatoes, sliced thickly
8	Marinated Tofu Steaks (see p. 90)
6 cups	cooked brown basmati rice (see p. 3)
1 batch	Miso Gravy (see p. 91)
1 bunch	cilantro, chopped
1 bunch	green onions, chopped
2 tbsp.	brown sesame seeds, toasted

Method

1. Grill the zucchini, tomatoes and tofu steaks in the oven at medium to high heat, until lightly browned.
2. Put 1 1/2 cups cooked brown basmati rice in a large rice bowl.
3. Pour one 4-ounce ladle of warm Miso Gravy over the rice.
4. Arrange the grilled vegetables and tofu steaks around the inner edges of the bowl.
5. Put chopped cilantro and green onions on the Miso Gravy at the centre of the bowl.
6. Garnish with toasted brown sesame seeds. Repeat for each serving.

Green Goddess Rice Bowl

Get your steamed greens and brown rice here. Sound a bit boring? Not if you have our version of it. This is a beautiful bowl of emerald-green steamed vegetables with a piquant tamari and ginger Simple Sauce, creamy Tahini Sauce, nori, toasted sunflower seeds and pickled ginger over brown rice. Very healthy and twice as delicious. For added protein top with the Marinated Tofu Steaks (see page 90) or Marinated Tempeh (see page 89).

Serves 4

Ingredients

1 head	broccoli, cut into florets
1 head	bok choy, torn
1 bunch	green kale, torn
1 bunch	swiss chard, torn
6 cups	cooked brown basmati rice (see p. 3)
1 batch	Tahini Sauce (see p. 98)
2 sheets	nori, torn
1/3 cup	sunflower seeds, toasted
1 batch	Simple Sauce (see p. 92)
1/2 cup	white pickled ginger

Method

1. Steam broccoli and greens until they are tender and bright green.
2. Put 1 1/2 cups cooked brown basmati rice in a large rice bowl. Drizzle 2 tablespoons of Tahini Sauce on the rice. Place nori pieces on rice.
3. Arrange the steamed greens and broccoli on the brown rice around the bowl. Sprinkle toasted sunflower seeds on top. Drizzle 2 tablespoons of Simple Sauce on the vegetables and rice.
4. Garnish with a small mound of pickled ginger on top. Repeat for each serving.

Free Tibet Rice Bowl

What does freeing Tibet have to do with food? Well, the saying goes that the way to a person's heart is through their stomach. My intention in naming this rice bowl the Free Tibet was to raise awareness on this topic. In my heart, I support the current Dalai Lama's pursuit of religious freedom for his people, the right of thousands of Tibetans to return from living in exile, and the preservation of their ancient customs. This rice bowl is truly delicious and quite simple to prepare. The special touch is the steamed spinach on top.

Serves 4

Ingredients

12 slices	**Marinated Tempeh (see p. 89)**
4	**large handfuls spinach, washed and chopped**
6 cups	**cooked brown basmati rice (see p. 3)**
1 batch	**Tahini Sauce (see p. 98)**
1/2 cup	**white pickled ginger**
4 tsp.	**tamari**
4 handfuls	**buckwheat sprouts**
4 tsp.	**sesame seeds, toasted**

Method

1. Grill or broil the Marinated Tempeh slices in the oven until brown on both sides, about 5 minutes.
2. Steam the spinach in a steamer or with water in a shallow pan.
3. Put 1 1/2 cups of cooked brown basmati rice in a large rice bowl. Drizzle 2 tablespoons of Tahini Sauce on the rice.
4. Place 3 slices of Marinated Tempeh on one side of the bowl and the pickled ginger on the other.
5. Pile a portion of the steamed spinach in the middle. Pour 1 teaspoon of tamari over the spinach. Pile a handful of buckwheat sprouts on top of the spinach.
6. Garnish with sesame seeds. Repeat for each serving.

Noodles

Noodles are the popular comfort food of the Far East. It's no wonder, as they are so versatile, inexpensive and easy to prepare. You can find dozens of noodles prepared in a variety of ways, served at roadside stalls, with the strong scent of sizzling garlic in the air. Our noodle dishes are accompanied by special sauces or spice mixtures (found in the Sauces and Marinades section). The sauces are easily frozen for later use. Wise women say, "Good noodles need good sauce to be great!"

Thai Noodles

You can make only two servings at a time even in a large wok, but this dish keeps its heat very well, so the first two will still be piping hot when the last two are done. Add a pinch of hot crushed chili peppers for a spicier dish.

Serves 4

Ingredients

6 cups	rice noodles
6 cups	chopped greens (mix of bok choy, swiss chard and green kale)
1 1/2 cups	Marinated Tofu Cubes (see p. 90)
1	tomato, chopped
1 batch	Thai Noodle Sauce (see p. 96)
2 cups	bean sprouts
1	lemon, cut into 4 wedges
1/2 bunch	cilantro, chopped
handful	roasted peanuts, chopped (optional)

Method

1. Soak the rice noodles in warm water for about 15 minutes, while you prepare the other ingredients.
2. In a wok, put half of the greens, tofu and tomato. Add half the amount of Thai Noodle Sauce. Bring to a boil; then reduce heat and simmer for 5 minutes, until greens are tender.
3. Toss half the soaked noodles with the above ingredients and continue to simmer until the noodles are soft, about 2 minutes.
4. Remove from heat and divide the noodles into 2 large bowls.
5. Garnish with fresh bean sprouts, a wedge of lemon and chopped cilantro. Roasted peanuts are also a tasty garnish.
6. Repeat with the remaining ingredients for your next 2 servings.

Sri Lankan Spaghetti

Sri Lanka is an island off the southern tip of India. This dish fuses exotic Far Eastern spices with pasta, the traditional food of Italy. Experiment with different noodles each time you prepare this. You can't go wrong.

Serves 4

Ingredients

4 tbsp.	olive oil
1	red pepper, cut into julienne slices
1	green pepper, cut into julienne slices
1/2	red onion, peeled and sliced into half moons
1	zucchini, cut into julienne slices
2	tomatoes, diced
8 tbsp.	lemon juice
8 tbsp.	tamari
1/2 tsp.	sea salt
1 batch	Sri Lankan Spice Mix (see p. 94)
8 cups	cooked spaghetti
1	small bunch cilantro, chopped
4	lemon wedges

Method

1. Heat the olive oil in a wok over medium to high heat. Add the vegetables (except one diced tomato), lemon juice, tamari and sea salt. Cook until vegetables are slightly softened, about 3 minutes.
2. Add 8 tablespoons of the Sri Lankan Spice Mix and stir to coat the vegetables. Cook for 2 more minutes.
3. Gently toss the spiced vegetables with the cooked spaghetti in a large mixing bowl.
4. Pile each serving of spaghetti onto a plate and garnish with cilantro, reserved chopped tomato and a lemon wedge.

Rainforest Stir-Fry

The spicy mango sauce mixed with fresh cilantro makes this dish a hit. Substitute soba noodles for rice noodles for a change.

Serves 4

Ingredients

4 tbsp.	olive oil
4 cups	tofu, cubed
2	tomatoes, cut in wedges
2	red onions, peeled and cut in wedges
4 heads	chopped baby bok choy
1 batch	Spicy Mango Sauce (see p. 93)
8 cups	cooked soba noodles
1	orange, sliced
1	green jalapeño, sliced
4	cilantro sprigs

Method

1. Heat 2 tablespoons of olive oil in a wok over high heat. Add 2 cups of the tofu cubes and let brown on all sides. Do not disturb the tofu too much when it's cooking or it will break up.
2. When the tofu is browned on all sides, add half of the tomato, onion and baby bok choy. Cook over high heat until vegetables are slightly browned but still crunchy and the tomato is softened.
3. Add 8 ounces of Spicy Mango Sauce and 4 cups of cooked soba noodles to the vegetables. Toss gently until heated through.
4. Garnish with sliced orange and jalapeño and a few sprigs of cilantro. Repeat for the next 2 servings.

Khao San Soba

I had a bowl of noodles just like this one for $1.50 on the famed Khao San Road in Bangkok. This road is a mecca for backpackers and budget travellers with its cheap accommodations and numerous curb-side cafés.

Serves 4

Ingredients

1 cup	cashew pieces
8 cups	cooked soba noodles
2 batches	Green Dressing (see p. 84)
2 heads	broccoli, cut in florets
2 cups	grated carrots

Method

1. Toast the cashews in the oven at 350° F until they begin to brown.
2. Heat half the amount of soba noodles, cashews and Green Dressing in a pan over medium heat until heated through, about 5 minutes. Toss gently to avoid tearing the noodles.
3. Steam half the broccoli florets separately in a vegetable steamer or a shallow pan of water.
4. Divide the noodles and pile onto 2 dinner plates. Arrange broccoli around perimeter of plate and garnish with grated carrots in the centre. Repeat for the next two servings.

Dressings

Let's face it, for most of us it's the dressing that makes eating salad a truly enjoyable experience. If you have a good dressing, you can eat all the greens you are supposed to and never get bored. However, too much oil, salt or saturated fat in a dressing can defeat your good intentions and sabotage your body's ability to digest the healthy salad you just ate. The following recipes don't sacrifice flavour for the sake of a healthy dressing. And they are really quick to make!

House Dressing New!

This delicious, light dressing started its life as Apple Cider Vinaigrette, but when it quickly became a staff favourite, we renamed it the House Dressing. Now it's everyone's favourite dressing. It goes perfectly with the California Classic Salad (see page 38).

Flax oil is available at health food stores and an increasing number of grocery stores in the refrigerated section. It has a mild nutty flavour and is high in Omega 3 fatty acids. Flax oil is said to be beneficial to our health in countless ways, from increasing cardiovascular and colon health, to boosting immunity, alleviating depression and promoting healthy skin. This delicate oil goes rancid quickly, so only buy it if it is refrigerated and packaged in a black container, and buy the smallest amount possible.

Makes 4 servings

Ingredients

1/4 cup	filtered water
1/4 cup	apple cider vinegar
1/4 tsp.	raw sugar
1 tsp.	lemon juice
2 tsp.	sea salt
3/4 tsp.	ground black pepper
3/4 tsp.	tamari
1/4 tsp.	mustard powder
1 clove	garlic
1/4 cup	flax oil
3/4 cup	sunflower oil

Method

In blender, mix all ingredients except oil until totally puréed. With blender running, add oil in a thin stream until dressing is emulsified.

Wasabi Dill Dressing New!

We find that it really makes a difference to the dressing if you mix the water and wasabi first, before adding any other ingredients. This method seems to wake up the wasabi. Otherwise, the wasabi flavour never seems to develop and will just get lost.

Store in a sealed container in the fridge. Keeps for up to three days.

Makes 4 servings

Ingredients

1 tbsp. & 1/4 cup	olive oil
1	onion, peeled and thinly sliced
3 cloves	garlic, minced
1 tbsp.	wasabi powder
6 tbsp.	filtered water
2 cups	firm tofu, chopped
1 tsp.	Dijon mustard
1 tbsp.	dried dill weed
1/4 cup	rice vinegar
1/4 tsp.	sea salt

Method

1. Heat 1 tablespoon of olive oil in frying pan over medium heat.
2. Sauté onion and garlic five minutes or until softened. Let cool.
3. Put wasabi and 2 tablespoons water into the blender and blend.
4. Add remaining ingredients and 2 tablespoons of water. Blend until smooth. Add remaining water if needed to get to a pourable consistency.

Balsamic Vinaigrette

This delicious, classic dressing takes literally 5 minutes to make once you have your ingredients laid out. You don't need to use expensive balsamic vinegar for this dressing, as it will be combined with other flavourful ingredients.

Makes 4 servings

Ingredients

4 tbsp.	balsamic vinegar
1 tbsp.	lemon juice
2 tbsp.	fresh or bottled apple juice
1 tsp.	Dijon mustard
1/2 tsp.	dry tarragon
1 pinch	sea salt
1 pinch	black pepper
2/3 cup	olive oil

Method

In a food processor or blender, combine the ingredients and process until emulsified.

Creamy Caesar Dressing

Hold the anchovies! Try this instead. A blender will give the proper consistency for this dressing. A food processor has trouble getting the tofu totally smooth.

Makes 4 servings

Ingredients

1 1/2 tbsp.	capers
2 cloves	garlic, minced
2 tbsp.	lemon juice

3/4 cup	tofu, chopped
2 1/2 tsp.	Dijon mustard
1 tbsp.	apple cider vinegar
1/2 tsp.	sea salt
3/4 tsp.	ground white pepper
1/4 cup	filtered water
1/2 cup	olive oil

Method

Put all the ingredients in a blender and process until smooth, scraping the sides down once or twice.

Creamy Sunflower Dressing

If you use less water in this dressing, you will get a tasty dip or spread for sandwiches. Add curry powder for a curried sunflower dip for vegetables.

Makes 4 servings

Ingredients

2/3 cup	raw sunflower seeds
3 cloves	garlic, minced
1/3 cup	grapefruit juice
3 tbsp.	lemon juice
1/2 tsp.	sea salt
1 cup	filtered water

Method

Combine all the ingredients in a blender or food processor. Process until dressing becomes thick, frothy and smooth, for about 2 minutes.

Green Dressing

This light dressing is a bright shade of green that looks great on a colourful salad like the Mega Life (see page 40). This dressing is also delicious served over noodles like the Khao San Soba (see page 77).

Makes 4 servings

Ingredients

2 cloves	garlic, minced
2 tsp.	peeled and chopped ginger root
1/4 cup	rice vinegar
1 1/4 cup	chopped cilantro
1/4 cup	filtered water
2 tbsp.	sunflower oil
1/4 tsp.	wasabi
2 tbsp.	honey

Method

Put the garlic, ginger, rice vinegar, cilantro and water in a blender. Process until smooth. Add remaining ingredients while the blender is running. Remove when fully liquified.

Sauces and Marinades

Some of these sauces, marinades and spices match specific dishes, but most can be used wherever you like them. Once you are familiar with the recipes and tastes, feel free to get creative and try the sauces in new and exciting ways. Stash's Hot Sauce will add kick to any dish, and Miso Gravy tastes good on just about everything.

Coconut Curry Sauce

The flavour of this sauce can be influenced by the type of curry you choose to use. At Fresh, we use an aromatic yellow Indian curry powder, often called a masala-style curry. When cooking at home, I also enjoy using a vindaloo-style Indian curry paste, which is darker and spicier.

Makes 6 servings

Ingredients

3 tbsp.	sunflower oil
1	onion, peeled and chopped
2 cloves	garlic
1/2 tsp.	cumin, ground
3/4 tsp.	sea salt
3 tbsp.	curry powder
3 tbsp.	spelt flour
3 cups	Vegetable Stock (see p. 20)
2 cups	coconut milk
3 large	tomatoes, diced

Method

1. Heat the sunflower oil in a saucepan over medium heat.
2. Add the onion and garlic. Cook for 5 minutes until soft.
3. Add spices and cook for 1 minute.
4. Add flour and cook for 1 minute.
5. Stir in the Vegetable Stock gradually to prevent lumps forming.
6. Add the coconut and tomatoes, stirring occasionally.
7. Simmer for half an hour.

Crispy Tofu Coating (New!)

Crispy Tofu is our most sought-after recipe. Those of you who have been asking for it will be surprised to discover how utterly simple it is! Kids love this recipe, too. Crispy Tofu cubes are fun to make at home and delicious as a topping for rice, noodles or salad. It has a certain down-home, southern-fried food taste that appeals to meat eaters and vegetarians alike.

This dry mix lasts indefinitely, as long as it doesn't have chunks of tofu or food left in it. It's a good idea to separate the amount of coating you need, so that if little bits of food break off, you won't contaminate the whole batch. This coating can be used on almost any food that has enough moisture to make the coating stick. At Fresh, we use it on Marinated Tofu Cubes (page 90), on Marinated Tofu Steaks (page 90), in the Ninja Rice Bowl (see page 67) and in the Magic Tofu Wrap (see page 54).

Makes 6 servings

Ingredients

1 cup	flaked nutritional yeast
1/2 cup	wheat germ
1 tbsp.	garlic powder
1/4 tsp.	sea salt
1/4 tsp.	black pepper

Method

Combine all the ingredients in a large bowl and mix well.

Garlic Dipping Sauce

This is a sweet and spicy dipping sauce served hot or cold.

Makes 10 servings

Ingredients

1 cup	raw sugar
3/4 cup	filtered water
1/4 cup	white vinegar
2 tbsp.	minced garlic
1 tsp.	sea salt
1 tbsp.	Stash's Hot Sauce (see p. 95)

Method

1. Combine all the ingredients except the hot sauce in a saucepan and cook over medium heat. Bring to a boil while stirring occasionally. Reduce heat and simmer for 20 minutes until the sauce thickens to the consistency of syrup.
2. Stir in the Hot Sauce and remove from heat.

Mango Cilantro Dipping Sauce (New!)

This is the fabulous light-tasting dipping sauce we serve with the Coconut Tempeh appetizer (see page 9).

Serves 4

Ingredients

1/4 cup	mango juice
1/4 cup	filtered water
1 clove	garlic, minced
1 tbsp.	chopped cilantro

1/2	lime, peeled and chopped
1/2 cup	rice vinegar
4 tbsp.	raw sugar
1/2 tsp.	crushed chilies

Method

Place all ingredients in a blender and process until smooth.

Marinated Tempeh

Tempeh is sold frozen in a solid block wrapped in plastic. To prepare it for marinating, remove the plastic and drop the tempeh into a pot of boiling water for 5 minutes until it thaws and softens. Be sure not to overcook the tempeh or it will break apart when it's marinating. Let the tempeh cool before you cut it into 1/4-inch-thick slices.

Makes 4 servings

Ingredients

2 tbsp.	filtered water
1/3 cup	tamari
1/3 cup	balsamic vinegar
1 tbsp.	sesame oil
1 tbsp.	sunflower oil
1 tsp.	white pepper
1 1/2 tsp.	ground anise
2 tsp.	garlic powder

Method

1. Mix all marinade ingredients in a bowl and then pour it over tempeh. Marinate for 1 hour before cooking or grilling.
2. Store in a sealed container. Keeps up to one week in the fridge.

Marinated Tofu Cubes

Contrary to widespread belief, tofu does indeed have a subtle taste. Taste and texture therefore vary from brand to brand. A good rule of thumb is to be sure to use a firm or extra-firm tofu. A firm tofu will hold its shape while marinating. This is a simple marinade that will add lots of delicious flavour to your raw tofu. Marinated Tofu Cubes require no cooking and can be served in a salad, in a wrap or as a rice bowl topping.

Makes 6 servings

Ingredients

3 1/2 cups	**tofu**
1/2 cup	**apple cider vinegar**
3/4 cup	**tamari**
1/4 cup	**filtered water**
1 1/2 tbsp.	**sunflower oil**

Method

1. Cut the tofu into medium-sized cubes.
2. Combine the remaining ingredients in a bowl; then pour over the tofu cubes. Marinate for 1 hour. Store in a sealed container in the fridge. Keeps up to 5 days.

Marinated Tofu Steaks

We call these tofu triangles "steaks" because they are char-grilled at Fresh and served warm over salads, rice bowls and in wraps. This is a great tofu marinade for the barbeque.

Makes 4 servings

Ingredients

1 block	**tofu**
2 tsp.	**coriander, ground**
4 tsp.	**garlic powder**
1/2 cup	**tamari**
2 cups	**filtered water**

Method

1. Cut the square block of tofu into 1/4-inch-thick slices; then cut the slices diagonally into triangles.
2. Combine the remaining ingredients in a bowl and pour over the tofu triangles. Marinate for 1 hour. Store in a sealed container in the fridge. Keeps up to 5 days.

Miso Gravy

Miso paste is available in most health food stores or Chinese grocery stores. The darker the miso, the more pungent the flavour. Once you have your ingredients measured out, this tasty gravy takes only 2 minutes to make. If you find that it is too thick, whisk in some water until you reach the desired consistency.

Makes 4 servings

Ingredients

4 1/2 tbsp.	spelt flour
1/4 tsp.	garlic powder
3/4 cup	Engevita (inactive) yeast
1 1/2 cups	Vegetable Stock (see p. 20) or filtered water
1/3 cup	sunflower oil
1 1/2 tsp.	Dijon mustard
3 tbsp.	miso paste, light or dark
3/4 tsp.	sea salt

Method

1. Put dry ingredients except salt in a saucepan over low heat. Whisk in the Vegetable Stock or water to make a paste.
2. Let this come to a boil and simmer for 30 seconds.
3. Add the oil, mustard, miso and salt to the ingredients in the saucepan. Whisk until everything is incorporated and the mixture is smooth. Serve hot. This recipe is used in the Dragon Rice Bowl (see p. 68) and the Miso Burger (see p. 59).

Ninja 2 Sauce

This spicy, salty sauce is what clinches the Ninja Rice Bowl (see page 67) as our most popular rice bowl currently. The rice mellows the intensity, so don't be shy using it.

Makes 8 servings

Ingredients

1/2 cup	**Simple Sauce (p. 92)**
1 tsp.	**Hot Sauce (p. 95)**

Method

Combine Simple Sauce and Hot Sauce in a bowl and mix well.

Simple Sauce

This intensely flavoured sauce is the secret ingredient responsible for the steady popularity of the Green Goddess Rice Bowl (see page 70). Only two tablespoons are needed for one rice bowl. Any extra will keep indefinitely in the fridge. Mixed with orange or mango juice, it makes a delicious stir-fry sauce.

Makes 4 servings

Ingredients

1/2 cup	**tamari**
3 tbsp.	**sesame oil**
1 1/2 inch	**ginger root, peeled and minced**
4 tbsp.	**lemon juice**

Method

Put all ingredients in a saucepan. Bring to a boil and let simmer for 10 minutes. Remove from heat and let cool.

Spicy Mango Sauce

We use Kikkoman mirin rice wine for seasoning and cooking. This common brand is widely available in Asian grocery stores and is a natural sweetener leaving a flavour and glaze on the ingredients that is ideal for stir-fries.

Makes 4 servings

Ingredients

2	jalapeños, sliced
3/4 cup	mirin rice wine
1/4 cup	tamari
1/2 cup	rice vinegar
1/4 cup	sunflower oil
1/4 cup	ketchup
1/4 cup	grapefruit juice
3/4 cup	bottled mango juice
1/4 cup	lemon juice
1/2 tsp.	sea salt
2 tbsp.	cornstarch
1/4 cup	filtered water
1/2 bunch	cilantro, chopped

Method

1. Combine all the ingredients except the cornstarch, water and cilantro in a medium saucepan.
2. Bring to a boil, reduce heat and let simmer for 20 minutes.
3. Combine the cornstarch and water in a small mixing bowl.
4. Whisk the cornstarch mixture into the simmering sauce. Let cook for 1 minute.
5. Add the chopped cilantro, cook 30 seconds more and remove from heat.

Sri Lankan Spice Mix

A spice grinder ensures the freshness and potency of the spices you are using. If you don't have one, buy the spices ground. This authentic spice mix can be used as a curry base for any number of soups, stews and rice dishes. There are many varieties of curries from all around the world. I love this Southern Indian curry because it features the exotic aroma of fennel, coriander and cardamom. For a spicier version, simply add some cayenne pepper.

Makes 4 servings

Ingredients

1 tbsp.	cumin seeds
1 tbsp.	fennel seeds
1 1/2 tsp.	cardamom seeds
8 tbsp.	coriander seeds
1 tbsp.	turmeric powder
4 tbsp.	chili powder
1 tbsp.	garlic powder
1 tsp.	cinnamon
1 tsp.	black peppercorns

Method

1. In a dry pan, toast the first four ingredients over low heat until they have slightly darkened and start to smell fragrant.
2. Add remaining ingredients to pan and toast for a minute or so until the powders change colour slightly. Be careful not to burn.
3. Remove from heat, let cool and then grind in spice grinder.

Stash's Hot Sauce

Stash is a real person, although his reputation has attained mythic proportions. A close friend and co-worker, he hails from Guyana and Trinidad and now lives in Costa Rica. This sauce has really great flavour and is very hot. It will store in the fridge for up to three months.

Makes 10 servings

Ingredients

4	scotch bonnet peppers
1/2	red onion, peeled and chopped
2	green onions, chopped
2 cloves	garlic
1/2 inch	ginger root
1 sprig	thyme
1 sprig	rosemary
1/2 cup	tamari
1/4 cup	balsamic vinegar
1 stalk	lemongrass
1/4 cup	Dijon mustard
1/2 tsp.	curry powder
1/2 tsp.	cayenne pepper
1/2 tsp.	crushed chilies
1/4 tsp.	oregano
1/4 tsp.	cinnamon
1/4 tsp.	cumin, ground

Method

1. Purée the first seven ingredients in a blender or food processor.
2. Put the puréed ingredients with the tamari in a pan. Cook over low heat until dark brown, about 5 minutes.
3. Add the rest of the ingredients and simmer for half an hour. Remove from heat. Store in a sealed container in the fridge.

Thai Noodle Sauce

This recipe requires a juicer or store-bought carrot juice.

Makes 4 servings

Ingredients

3 inches	ginger root, chopped
12 cloves	garlic
1/3 cup	sesame oil
2/3 cup	raw sunflower seeds
1 1/3 cup	grated coconut
2 tbsp.	chili powder
2/3 cup	lemon juice
2/3 cup	tamari
5 cups	carrot juice
2 tsp.	sea salt
4 tsp.	paprika
1 stalk	lemongrass, one end cut off and smashed to release fragrance

Method

1. In a food processor, purée the ginger and garlic.
2. Heat the sesame oil in a saucepan over medium heat. Add the puréed ginger and garlic and cook for 5 minutes.
3. In the food processor, grind the sunflower seeds to a coarse meal.
4. Put the ground sunflower seeds and the rest of the ingredients into the saucepan.
5. Bring ingredients to a boil, reduce heat and simmer for 30 minutes.
6. Remove the stalk of lemongrass.

Thai Peanut Sauce

Be very careful when heating this sauce, as the peanut butter burns easily. If it becomes too thick or separates, just whisk in some water or stock until it is the right consistency. If you have a juicer, you can replace the Vegetable Stock with carrot and celery juice for a deeper, fuller flavour. Stores for up to one week in the fridge.

Makes 4 servings

Ingredients

5 cloves	garlic, minced
1 inch	ginger root, peeled and minced
1 1/2 cups	natural smooth peanut butter
3/4 cup	lemon juice
5 tbsp.	tamari
2 tbsp.	paprika
2 cups	Vegetable Stock (see p. 20) or filtered water
	cayenne pepper to taste

Method

1. Combine all the ingredients in a bowl and whisk until smooth.
2. Heat gently for 10 minutes, stirring often. Serve hot.

Tahini Sauce

Sesame butter is also called raw tahini and is the base for this sauce and dressing. This is the sauce you traditionally would find in Lebanese food like falafel. It is a popular condiment at Fresh. Try a dash of tamari with it. It is often ordered with a side of Green Dressing (see page 84) and combined over a salad.

Makes 4 servings

Ingredients

2 cloves	garlic, minced
1/2 cup	chopped parsley
1/2 tsp.	sea salt
2 tbsp.	lemon juice
2/3 cup	filtered water
1/2 cup	sesame butter (tahini)

Method

Whiz garlic, parsley, salt and lemon juice in a blender or food processor. Add the water and sesame butter. Run until smooth, scraping the sides down once or twice.

Spreads and Fillings

You'll find that our fillings are the base for a number of recipes. The Black Bean Filling can be found in the Black Bean Burrito, while the Curried Garbanzo Filling is used in the Indian Dosas and the Kathmandu Wrap. Hummus can be used as a spread, a filling or even a dip for fresh veggies.

Black Bean Filling

The popularity of our Black Bean Burrito (see page 50) hinges on this tasty filling. Increase the amount of cayenne pepper for added spiciness. It also doubles as a filling for quesadillas or as a warm dip for corn chips.

Makes 6 servings

Ingredients

6 tbsp.	olive oil
2	onions, peeled and diced
4 cloves	garlic, minced
2 tsp.	cumin seeds, toasted and ground
1 tsp.	cayenne pepper
2 tsp.	apple cider vinegar
1 tsp.	sea salt
4 cups	canned or cooked black beans

Method

1. Heat the oil over medium heat in a saucepan. Add onions and cook for 5 minutes until soft.
2. Add the remaining ingredients except the black beans. Simmer for 5 minutes.
3. While that is cooking, purée the black beans in a food processor or mash as smoothly as possible by hand.
4. Add black beans to mixture. Stir until heated through.

Curried Garbanzo Filling

This recipe is very versatile. Use it as a filling for wraps or as a rice bowl topping. We use it in the Indian Dosas (see page 11), the Kathmandu Wrap (see page 49) and the Energy Rice Bowl (see page 66). Be careful not to touch your face, especially your eyes, while chopping the banana chilies, and wash your hands carefully after.

Makes 6 servings

Ingredients

2 tbsp.	olive oil
5 cloves	garlic, crushed
1	onion, peeled and finely diced
1	carrot, peeled and finely diced
1	green pepper, finely diced
2 medium	hot banana chilies, minced
2 tbsp.	cumin, ground
1 tbsp.	oregano
1 tbsp.	sea salt
1 tbsp.	turmeric
4 cups	cooked or canned chick peas
1/2 cup	tomato paste

Method

1. Heat the olive oil in a large saucepan. Add the garlic, spices and vegetables. Cook the mixture over medium to low heat until soft.
2. Mash the chick peas in a food processor or by hand, and add to saucepan along with tomato paste.
3. Stir until heated through.

Herb Tofu Mayo

This is our original, classic mayo. This healthy mayo goes beautifully in sandwiches, wraps and burgers.

Makes 6 servings

Ingredients

2 cups	firm tofu
1 clove	garlic, minced
1 tbsp.	apple cider vinegar
1 tsp.	Dijon mustard
1 tsp.	sea salt
1/2 tsp.	ground white pepper
1/4 cup	filtered water
1 tbsp.	sunflower oil
3 tbsp.	Mixed Dry Herbs (see p. 5)

Method

1. In a food processor, whiz the tofu, garlic and apple cider vinegar until smooth. Scrape down the sides of the bowl.
2. Add remaining ingredients and process until smooth, scraping down the sides of the bowl periodically.

House Mayo (New!)

Formerly known as our Honey Mustard Mayo, we recently updated this recipe to make it totally vegan.

Serves 6

Ingredients

1/2	onion, peeled and chopped
1 clove	garlic, minced
2 tsp.	white cooking wine
1 pinch	sea salt
1 pinch	nutmeg
1 pinch	ground black pepper
1/4 tsp.	Mixed Dry Herbs (see p. 5)
4 tbsp.	Vegetable Stock (see p. 20)
2 tsp.	miso paste
1 cup	firm tofu, chopped
2 tsp.	Dijon mustard
1 tbsp.	raw sugar
3 tbsp.	sunflower oil
2 tsp.	apple cider vinegar

Method

1. Combine onion, garlic, wine, salt, nutmeg, pepper, herbs and stock in a frying pan and cook over medium heat until liquid has evaporated, stirring occasionally.
2. Remove from heat and allow to cool.
3. Combine onion mixture, miso, tofu, mustard, sugar, oil and vinegar in a blender and blend until totally smooth. You may need to add a little water depending on the firmness of the tofu in order to get a mayo-like consistency.

Hummus

There is no end to the variations you can try when making this at home. You can add fresh herbs and roasted red peppers to the mixture. Hummus makes a delicious starter with a side of grilled pita and black olives. To garnish, mix one teaspoon of olive oil with a pinch of paprika and drizzle the red liquid onto the hummus.

Makes 6 servings

Ingredients

2 cups	cooked or canned chick peas
3 cloves	garlic, minced
2 tbsp.	raw tahini
4 tbsp.	lemon juice
1/2 tsp.	sea salt
1 tbsp.	filtered water

Method

1. In a food processor, purée all the ingredients.
2. Add water gradually to reach the consistency you prefer.
3. Store in a sealed container in the fridge. Keeps for up to a week.

Spinach Basil Pesto

When fresh basil is out of season and expensive, increase the amount of spinach you use in this recipe. During the summer months, we buy bushels of fresh basil to make pesto to freeze for the winter months.

Makes 6 servings

Ingredients

2 cloves	garlic, minced
1 tsp.	sea salt
1/4 cup	sunflower seeds
1/3 cup	pine nuts
3 tbsp.	olive oil
1 bunch	fresh basil, stems removed
2 cups	chopped fresh spinach

Method

1. Blend the garlic, sea salt, pine nuts, sunflower seeds and olive oil in a blender or food processor until smooth.
2. Mix in the fresh basil and spinach. Scrape down the sides once or twice.
3. Store in a sealed container in the fridge or freezer.

Marinated Sundried Tomato Paste

If you love sundried tomatoes and use them often, this is a great recipe to help them go a little further. A thin layer of this piquant paste will perk up the dullest of sandwiches. To make the marinated sundried tomatoes that we use in the Ninja Rice Bowl (see page 67) and the Big Sur Salad (see page 45), just follow the first two steps of this recipe.

Makes 6 servings

Ingredients

1 cup	filtered water
1 cup	sundried tomatoes
1 cup	olive oil
2 tbsp.	Mixed Dry Herbs (see p. 5)

Method

1. Bring water to a boil in a saucepan. Remove from heat and add the sundried tomatoes. Let sit for 5 minutes or until softened. Strain.
2. In a bowl, mix the olive oil and herbs together. Stir in the sundried tomatoes.
3. Purée in a blender or food processor. Scrape down the sides once or twice.
4. Store in a sealed container in the fridge.

Tofu Sour Cream (New!)

A dollop of this great-tasting vegan sour cream on a bowl of Red Bean and Lager Chili (see page 31) is the answer to the winter blues.

Ingredients

2 cups	firm tofu, chopped
3 tbsp.	sunflower oil
3 tbsp. + 1 tsp.	fresh lemon juice
1 tbsp.	raw sugar
1/2 tsp.	sea salt
2 tbsp.	filtered water

Method

Combine all ingredients in a blender and blend until completely smooth. Add more water if necessary to get the desired consistency.

Brunch

A vegan brunch is a thing of wonder and amazement to many people.
How do you make French toast without eggs? Or pancakes without milk and butter?

These special secrets are revealed here for your pleasure and use. You will be happy to discover that
these recipes are neither complicated nor difficult to prepare and the results are really scrumptious.
Our fabulous brunch recipes won't make you feel like going back to sleep when you are finished.
In fact, why wait for the weekend to have a really good breakfast?

Vegan Pancakes

These pancakes are scrumptious served with Fresh Fruit Sauce (see page 113) and a dollop of Tofu Whipped Cream (see page 112). Or try Toasted Nuts and Seeds (see page 4) with maple syrup.

Serves 6

Ingredients

Dry Mix

3 cups	**whole wheat pastry flour**
1 1/2 cups	**unbleached white flour**
3/4 cups	**bran**
2 tbsp.	**baking powder**
3/4 tsp.	**sea salt**

Wet Mix

4 tbsp.	**maple syrup**
1 tbsp.	**raw tahini**
4 tbsp.	**sunflower oil**
4 1/2 cups	**vanilla soymilk**
2	**bananas, sliced (optional)**

Method

1. Mix the dry ingredients and the wet ingredients (except banana) separately; then fold together with a whisk or large spoon. Be careful not to over-mix the batter. A few lumps in the batter are fine. Let stand for 5 minutes.
2. Heat a tablespoon of sunflower oil in a heavy-bottomed frying pan or skillet with a non-stick surface. Scoop 4 ounces of pancake batter and drop onto the hot surface.
3. Flip the pancake when the bottom side is brown and the batter on the top side is bubbling.
4. For banana pancakes, press several chunks of banana onto the side facing up in the pan. Flip over and cook until brown. Serve facing up.

French Toast

This French toast works best with a soft white bread hand sliced thickly and topped with Fresh Fruit Sauce (see page 113). Try it with our Tofu Whipped Cream (see page 112).

Serves 4

Ingredients

3 1/2 cups	firm tofu
2 tbsp.	vanilla extract
1/2 cup	honey
1 cup	plain soymilk
8 slices	bread, half-inch-thick slices
2 tbsp.	sunflower oil

Method

1. Mix the tofu, vanilla extract, honey and soymilk in a blender until smooth.
2. Put the batter in a bowl that is wide enough to dip your bread into.
3. Heat a small amount of sunflower oil in a frying pan over low heat.
4. Dip both sides of the bread into the batter and place in the pan.
5. Cook over medium to low heat until golden brown on both sides, about 5 minutes.

Tofu Whipped Cream

This can be used wherever you would normally use whipped cream. Using a blender rather than a food processor will guarantee a smooth consistency. We recommend it as a topping for French toast, pancakes or granola. I recently prepared this cream extra thick by using less soymilk, and layered it in a fresh fruit pie. It was delicious!

Makes 6 servings

Ingredients

3 1/2 cups	firm tofu
2 tsp.	vanilla extract
4 tbsp.	honey or maple syrup
1 tsp.	salt
2 tbsp.	vanilla soymilk

Method

1. Combine all ingredients in a blender and run until smooth for about 5 minutes.
2. Place in the refrigerator for 20 minutes to thicken and cool. If it is too thick, add a little more soymilk until you reach the right consistency.

Fresh Fruit Sauce

Blueberries, strawberries or peaches make ideal fruit sauce for pancakes or French toast. You may not need to sweeten the fruit sauce at all if the fruit is ripe. I've recently fallen in love with agave nectar, a mild natural sweetener that is made from the juice of the agave cactus plant. It has a low glycemic index, is easy to pour and dissolves quickly. Try it instead of honey or maple syrup to sweeten your fruit sauce. It's also nice in a hot cup of tea. Agave nectar is readily available in most health food stores.

Makes 6 servings

Ingredients

6 cups	**fruit (fresh or frozen)**
1/2 cup	**honey or maple syrup**
1/8 cup	**water**

Method

1. Put the ingredients in a saucepan and cook over medium heat, stirring occasionally, for about 15 minutes.
2. Serve hot.

Fresh Granola (New!)

We serve this hearty high-protein granola during our busy weekend brunches at the Fresh restaurants. This granola tastes delicious with all types of milk such as almond, rice, oat or soy. "Original" flavour is best, as it is the least sweetened of the non-dairy milks. Top with a non-dairy soy yogurt and fresh berries. Our Fresh Granola is also a key ingredient in the Ripped Power Shake (see page 159). This granola will keep for months in an airtight container.

Ingredients

1 tbsp.	sunflower oil
2 tsp.	maple syrup
1/4 cup	apple juice
1/4 tsp.	pure vanilla extract
2 1/2 cups	rolled oats
1/4 cup	raw pecans, chopped
1/4 cup	raw sunflower seeds, hulled
1/4 cup	raw almonds, chopped or sliced
1 tbsp.	hemp seeds, hulled
1/4 cup	raw cashews, chopped
1/4 cup	raw walnuts, chopped
1/8 cup	shredded coconut
1/4 cup	raw pumpkin seeds, hulled
1/8 cup	raisins
1/8 cup	currants
1/8 cup	dried apricots, chopped

Method

1. Preheat oven to 350° F.
2. In small bowl mix maple syrup, apple juice, vanilla and oil.
3. In large bowl mix oats, nuts, seeds and coconut. Add maple syrup mixture and toss to coat.
4. Spread mixture on a baking tray and cook until crispy, stirring often.
5. Let cool.
6. Add raisins, currants and apricots, stir and serve.

Savoury Scrambled Tofu

You can roll this mixture into a tortilla wrap like the Breakfast Burrito (see page 116), or you can eat it like a plate of scrambled eggs with toast, home fries and a grilled tomato.

Serves 4

Ingredients

1 tbsp.	olive oil
1	onion, peeled and chopped
3 cloves	garlic, minced
3 1/2 cups	tofu
3 tbsp.	Engevita (inactive) yeast
2 tsp.	dill weed
2 tsp.	garlic powder
1 pinch	turmeric
1 1/2 tsp.	sea salt
1 tsp.	black pepper
1/2 cup	filtered water

Method

1. Heat the olive oil in a saucepan over medium heat. Add onion and garlic and sauté until translucent.
2. Crumble the tofu with your hands and add to the pan. Cook for 2 minutes.
3. Combine the yeast, dill, garlic powder, turmeric, sea salt and black pepper in a small bowl with just enough water to form a thin sauce. Whisk with a fork to remove all lumps.
4. Pour this mixture onto your tofu and stir frequently. The turmeric will give the tofu a nice golden glow. Cook until all liquid has evaporated. Remove from heat.

Breakfast Burrito

This warm breakfast wrap makes a good lunch, too.

Serves 4

Ingredients

1 package	tofu sausages, sliced
2 cups	sliced mushrooms
1	green pepper, sliced
1	red pepper, sliced
1 batch	Savoury Scrambled Tofu (see p. 115)
4	10-inch whole wheat tortillas
1	tomato, sliced

Method

1. Sauté the sliced sausage and vegetables in a frying pan.
2. When they are cooked to your liking, add the scrambled tofu and stir until heated through.
3. Heat the tortilla in the oven or on a grill.
4. Grill or fry two slices of tomato.
5. Place the Scrambled Tofu mixture down the centre of the tortilla. Fold the edges in and roll up.
6. Garnish the plate with the grilled tomato and serve. Repeat for each serving.

Tofu Omelette

This omelette is the filling for the Wild Western Sandwich (see page 118), but you can also enjoy it folded over sautéed vegetables of your choice and served with a side salad.

Serves 6

Ingredients

2 tsp.	olive oil
1/2	onion, peeled and sliced
1/2 cup	grated carrot
1/2 cup	chopped scallions
3 cloves	garlic
3 1/2 cups	firm tofu, chopped
1 1/2 tbsp.	Engevita (inactive) yeast
1/2 cup	gluten flour
1 1/2 tsp.	sea salt
1 1/2 tsp.	black pepper
4 tbsp.	flour for dusting surface

Method

1. In a frying pan, heat the olive oil over medium heat. Add the sliced onion to the pan and reduce heat to low. Cook until onion is browned, about 10 minutes. Let cool.
2. In a food processor, put the browned onions, grated carrot, scallions and garlic. Process until smooth.
3. Add tofu and process with the other ingredients. Mix in remaining ingredients, except the dusting flour. Check the consistency of the mixture. It should be firm and easy to handle.
4. On a generously floured surface, pat out some of the mixture to about the size of a 6-inch dinner plate, about 1/2 inch thick. Repeat.
5. In a large flat-bottomed frying pan or skillet, heat 1 tablespoon of sunflower oil, just enough to cover the bottom of the pan. Place the round pancake in the pan. Cook until brown on both sides. Repeat for the remaining patties.

Wild Western Sandwich

You can serve this breakfast sandwich with House Mayo (see page 103) or ketchup. I like to use either Heinz or Muir Glen organic ketchups. They both use great-tasting, vine-ripened tomatoes and are only mildly sweetened. Try a nice green salad on the side, too.

Serves 6

Ingredients

1 batch	Tofu Omelette (see p. 117)
1 tbsp.	olive oil
1	onion, sliced
1	green pepper, sliced
1	red pepper, sliced
3 cups	button mushrooms, sliced
12 slices	multigrain bread, toasted
2	tomatoes, sliced

Method

1. Prepare Tofu Omelette. Set aside.
2. In a frying pan, heat the olive oil over medium heat. Sauté the onion for 1 minute.
3. Add the peppers and mushrooms and sauté another 5 minutes. Remove from heat.
4. Distribute the vegetables evenly on top of each omelette.
5. Fold each omelette over the vegetables and place between 2 slices of toasted bread with a slice or two of tomato. You may want to use toothpicks to hold the sandwiches together.

Chocolate Chip Spelt Muffins

These admittedly dense muffins make a delicious mid-morning or mid-afternoon snack for the active youngster or adult.

Makes 16 muffins

Ingredients

2 cups	soymilk, plain
1 1/3 cups	canola oil
2 cups	Date Purée (see p. 6)
1 cup	dark chocolate chips
6 cups	light spelt flour
4 tbsp.	baking powder
1 1/2 tsp.	sea salt

Method

1. Preheat oven to 325° F. Lightly spray or oil two regular-sized muffin trays.
2. In a large mixing bowl, combine all the ingredients to form a batter.
3. Scoop 1/2 cup of batter per muffin onto the tray.
4. Bake for 20 to 25 minutes. Let the muffins cool for 10 minutes before removing from trays. Store at room temperature or freeze in an air-tight container.

Banana Muffins

You can substitute two cups blueberries for the bananas in this recipe. Just add four more cups of water. Ripe bananas will give you a sweeter, moister muffin.

Makes 16 muffins

Ingredients

2 cups	rolled oats
4 cups	durum flour
1 cup	Date Purée (see p. 6)
3 1/4 tbsp.	baking powder
1 tsp.	baking soda
1 1/2 tsp.	sea salt
1 tsp.	cinnamon
1/2 tsp.	nutmeg
1 tsp.	vanilla extract
1 cup	canola oil
6	ripe bananas, mashed
2 cups	water

Method

1. Preheat oven to 325° F. Lightly spray or oil two regular-sized muffin trays.
2. In a large mixing bowl, combine all the ingredients to form a batter.
3. Scoop 1/2 cup of batter per muffin onto the tray.
4. Bake for 40 to 45 minutes. Let the muffins cool for 10 minutes before removing from trays. Store at room temperature or freeze in an air-tight container.

Maple Pecan Cookies

You can substitute walnuts or almonds for the pecans in this recipe.

Makes 32 wheat-free cookies

Ingredients

2 1/2 cups	maple syrup
1 cup	canola oil
1 1/2 cups	pecan halves
5 cups	barley flour
2 tsp.	cinnamon
1/2 tsp.	sea salt
1/2 cup	apple butter

Method

1. Combine all ingredients except the apple butter, stirring well. Add the flour gradually to avoid clumping.
2. Using a teaspoon, scoop the batter in portions (a rounded teaspoon) onto a waxed cookie sheet.
3. Press your thumb into the centre of each cookie. Fill the resulting dent with a dollop of apple butter.
4. Bake for 15 to 20 minutes at 325° F until the cookies begin to brown. Remove from heat even if the cookies are still a bit soft; they will harden as they cool.

Chocolate Brownie Cookies

This is a double-chocolate melt-in-your-mouth cookie. Make a batch and freeze half for later—otherwise, you may end up eating them all before you know it.

Makes 32 wheat-free cookies

Ingredients

2 1/2 cups	maple syrup
1 cup	canola oil
1 1/2 cups	dark chocolate chips
2 1/2 cups	dark cocoa
5 cups	barley flour
1/4 tsp.	sea salt
2 tsp.	vanilla extract

Method

1. Combine the syrup, oil and chocolate chips in a bowl.
2. In a separate bowl, combine the cocoa powder and barley flour.
3. Combine the two mixtures in a large bowl. Slowly add the remaining ingredients.
4. Using a teaspoon, scoop the batter in portions (a rounded teaspoon) onto a waxed cookie sheet. Slightly flatten each ball of dough with the back of the spoon.
5. Bake for 15 to 20 minutes at 350° F. Remove from heat even if the cookies are still a bit soft; they will harden as they cool.

Luscious Juice

Getting Juiced

Imagine getting intoxicated on fresh juice, feeling great and never having a hangover again. Imagine drinking a stream of super power shakes, energy and immune elixirs, exotic fruit smoothies and vegetable cocktails that leave you glowing, very much alive and kicking.

Luscious Juice gives you the opportunity to enhance your diet, health and present lifestyle with the inclusion of fresh juices, superfood supplements, protein powders and herbal tinctures. One step further and these juices can infiltrate your life to the exclusion of other vices you may have. The Super Energy Cocktail will replace your morning cup of coffee, and the Ripped Power Shake will supersede that beer you were about to order. Who needs Coke when you can have a Supersonic Energy Elixir? I consider my daily devotion to drinking fresh-squeezed fruit and vegetable juices a healthy addiction. Today, my idea of reckless drinking is a Rocket Fuel with a shot of organic espresso, while decadent relaxation is a ZenMatcha Power Shake, and an intense energy rush is a Liquid Oxygen with an ounce of wheatgrass.

Fresh fruit and vegetable juices have the power of nature's healing properties and nutritional building blocks to bring you closer to better health and well-being than you've ever been before. They are a rich, concentrated source of nutrients and give an instant boost of vital energy. The vitamins, minerals and enzymes present in live juices are absorbed much more quickly, easily and efficiently than whole foods that can take hours to digest. The quick and easy assimilation of fresh juices is due to the presence of live enzymes in raw fruits and vegetables. These enzymes are destroyed when fruits and vegetables are cooked. In today's busy world, when it seems there's never enough time to eat properly, juicing can ensure that your body gets the nourishment it needs to stay on top—fast. This is especially important for your immune system, which is constantly fending off assaults from bacteria, viruses, environmental toxins and stress.

You can use Luscious Juice as your inspiration and reference guide. Allow yourself to improvise and deviate from the ingredients, tailoring our juices to suit your needs. Let your senses lead you to your dream juice, and then let your body guide you to a new level of well-being.

Juicing Tips

At Fresh, we use high-output, centrifugal industrial juice extractors. One of our juicers, called a Santos, has a screen with small holes and a blade with tiny teeth for grinding that is used mainly for juicing fine, leafy greens and all vegetables. The other, called a Ruby, has a screen with larger holes and a knife-like blade, which is better for juicing wet fruits. These juicers separate the juice and eject the pulp into a bin outside the machine. This allows us to juice all day long, having to stop only occasionally to empty the bin. These powerful juicers produce a rich smooth juice. When juicing at home, you do not need such powerful high-output machines. Instead, choose a home juicer that suits you.

Buying a Juicer

Don't become one of the many people who have enthusiastically bought juicers and then given up because their juicer was such a chore to use and clean.

Consider these juicer questions:

1. **Is the juicer capable of producing the quantity and variety of juice you plan on making before you have to pause and clean it?**

   Several types of affordable juice extractors that can juice both fruits and vegetables are for sale in health food stores, restaurant equipment stores or online. I would highly recommend a centrifugal juicer for home use. Centrifugal juicers are highly efficient and easier to clean. A centrifuge holds the pulp inside the basket in order to continue to spin the pulp. Much like a washing machine on the spin cycle, a centrifugal juicer will spin the pulp, and extract and drain the juice out. For higher volume and greater efficiency, look for pulp ejection, which ejects the pulp into a separate container.

2. **Is this machine efficient? Is the juice pulpy or smooth?**

   It should be smooth since you don't want to chew your juice. Check the extracted pulp to see if it's dry or still moist with juice. The drier the pulp, the more juice in the glass. In the long run, an efficient juicer will save you money on the amount of produce you buy.

3. **Is it quick and easy to take apart, clean and reassemble?**

   Beware of little nooks and corners that are hard to reach and small parts that can easily get lost and are often hard to replace.

4. **How big, loud and heavy is it?**

Consider if there is room for it on your counter where you can see it (if you can see it, you're more likely to use it), if it's quiet enough not to disturb your housemates in the morning, and if you can travel with it.

The following juicers meet the above-mentioned criteria for efficient and fun home juicing. Google these juicers and you will find even more information as well as many online companies with large selections of juicers for sale.

The **Breville Juice Fountain Plus** is moderately priced at $175. It has an 850-watt two-speed motor that adjusts automatically to the juicing load. The ultra-quiet low speed is used for soft fruits such as watermelon, and the high speed is for juicing hard fruits and vegetables such as carrots or apples.

At $350, the **Breville Juice Fountain Elite** is twice the price of the Plus model, but it has a more powerful motor at 1000 watts and an extra-large stainless steel feed chute. A bigger feed chute means less prepping time and faster juicing. And, for what it's worth, it looks very good on the counter.

The **Omega Model 4000** is priced at $250. It is a very reliable centrifugal juicer with pulp ejection and a large feed chute. It has a 250-watt 1/3 horsepower motor with a stainless steel blade and basket. It is very easy to disassemble and easy to clean.

The **Omega 8003 or 8005** is priced at $300 and is a low-speed masticating juicer that can juice all the same hard or soft produce as a centrifugal juicer. However, it also has the ability to juice wheatgrass, which the others don't. A masticating juicer has a stone mill-like auger or gear that operates at low speeds, thus generating less friction and heat. This preserves the live enzymes and produces a juice that is somewhat higher in nutritional value. However, it is a much slower process.

The **L'Equip 221** at $200 is a very attractive juicer with all the bells and whistles that the Brevilles have. It has a computer-controlled motor that automatically supplies more or less power as needed, a stainless steel bowl and basket, a large feed chute and pulp ejection for continuous juicing.

The **Mini-L'Equip 110.5** at $120 is a really smart compact version of the 221 for your first juicer. The compact size works well on kitchen counters with limited space. It has a cool modern look to it.

The Sequence of Juicing

The key to successful juicing is to begin with the ingredients that have the lowest water content and end with ingredients with a higher water content. Ingredients with low water content such as garlic, ginger, parsley, spinach, red pepper and beets have a high concentration of flavour locked in their pulp. A juice extractor will separate the juice from the pulp but most of the juice will stay in the bowl unless you drive it out with an ingredient that has a higher water content such as carrot, celery, cucumber or apple. By flushing out the strongest flavours first, followed by the more neutral ingredients, you are ensuring that your next juice will not be tainted. Using a neutral ingredient last also allows you to adjust the flavour and potency of the drink.

Fresh-Squeezed Juice vs. Bottled Juice

The live enzymes and nutrients available in fresh-squeezed juices are not present in bottled juices. The nutritional value of store-bought bottled juice is dramatically reduced because enzymes are destroyed in the processing needed to bring it to the shelf. The closer you can stay to fresh juice, the greater the vitamin and mineral content that remains intact. Nevertheless, you will find a growing number of quality fruit juices in grocery and health food stores. If I am travelling or have little time to juice, I will blend fresh whole fruits, like bananas or frozen berries, with my favourite supplement and bottled fruit juice or soymilk. Black River, Ceres, Crofter's or Sarah's make a variety of high-quality natural unsweetened fruit juices. My favourites are mango, pomegranate, pear or apple. The trick is to check the labels to avoid added sugars, concentrates or preservatives.

Basic Juices

Basic juices act as the liquifying ingredient and base in the vegetable cocktail or smoothie. The fruits and vegetables used for the basic juices have a high water content that separates easily from the pulp (with the exception of pomegranate and mango, which we buy bottled). These juices enhance and balance the concentrated flavours and strong effects of other ingredients. A basic juice can stand alone or in combination with other juices. If you don't have a juicer, you will find most of these basic juices available bottled or frozen at your local health food store.

We have seven **basic fruit juices**: pineapple, orange, grapefruit, watermelon, pomegranate, mango, apple and pear. These juices get blended with whole soft fruits such as banana, kiwi, peach or berries to make a smoothie. Add a supplement, herbal tincture, soymilk or rice milk and voila, you have an energy elixir, immune elixir or power shake. All the basic fruit juices, excluding apple and pear, last easily up to 48 hours refrigerated in a sealed container. To save yourself preparation time, juice a little extra for the next couple of days and store in the fridge.

There are three **basic vegetable juices**: carrot, celery and cucumber. These vegetables are juiced in combination with more concentrated ingredients such as ginger, garlic, beet or parsley to create vegetable cocktails. Add an ounce of wheatgrass, spirulina, green drink powder like Greens+ or an herbal tincture to create an energy or immune elixir. Although vegetable juice will not spoil if refrigerated, the flavour, colour and potency will decline with oxidization. This is not juice you can buy bottled or prepare in advance.

Juicy Fruits

Orange, grapefruit and lemon are easy to juice if you peel them first and run them through your centrifugal juice extractor. I find this method creates a better yield, producing a smoother, less pulpy juice than the automatic hand juicers. In the centrifugal juice extractor, 1 medium orange yields approximately 4 ounces of juice and 1 medium grapefruit yields approximately 6 ounces of juice. Thin-skinned oranges like Florida Valencia tend to be juicier and sweeter. Get the larger size so you don't have to peel as many to make your juice. I like to use pink grapefruit, generally from Mexico, for its sweetness, colour and size.

Pineapple is very fibrous and needs water to flush it through the juicer. Not much—just add three ounces with every three or four slices. Use filtered water if you can. Four slices of pineapple will yield approximately 6 ounces of juice.

Watermelon is a dream to juice. If you don't have a juicer, you can liquify the watermelon slices in the blender. Just remove the peel and the seeds. If you're juicing the watermelon, you don't have to worry about the seeds; just peel the watermelon and run the slices through the juicer. Watermelon is mostly water and consequently produces a lot of juice. One slice yields approximately 6 ounces of juice.

Washing, Peeling, Seeding, Cutting

Wash your produce with a biodegradable soap to remove any sprays or pesticide residue. Use a vegetable brush to scrub the surfaces of your produce. Rinse them well before juicing. Do not soak produce in water as it will leach out the vitamins and minerals. Waxed cucumber and apple skins should be removed.

Peel citrus fruits when you use a centrifugal juice extractor. The citrus peel is bitter, and even a little bit left on the fruit will taint your juice. If you are using a hand juicer, make sure not to press all the way to the peel or your juice will have a bitter aftertaste.

Be sure to seed fruits such as peaches or plums that have large pits. Don't worry about apples, pears or watermelon; a centrifugal juicer will spit these smaller seeds out.

Cut your ingredients to fit the size of your juicer's hopper. Some hoppers are very narrow and require all produce to be cut small so the pieces will fit. Consider the size of your hopper when you are buying produce such as carrots and apples that come in different sizes. Parsley and spinach can be bunched into a handful for juicing.

The Dilemma of Organics

Conventional fruits and vegetables are sprayed with pesticides, herbicides and other harmful toxic substances. Whenever possible, it is wise to avoid conventional produce and instead buy organic, unsprayed produce. Seasonal availability, cost and quality are the determining factors in how much organic produce we buy. With organics, the improvement in texture and flavour, and the peace of mind are worth it. However, going organic doesn't always mean fresher produce. Apply the same criteria of quality and value to organic produce that you would to conventional produce. To get the best quality, buy locally farmed organic fruits and vegetables when they are in season.

Sipping, Not Gulping

Good digestion begins in the mouth. When you lay your eyes on attractive food that smells delicious, your body begins preparing to receive it. As your mouth waters in anticipation, it secretes digestive juices and enzymes ready to begin the process of assimilation and absorption. This is why slowly sipping, not gulping, your juice before you swallow is so important. As you swallow the juice with your saliva, its revitalizing nutrients are already being digested and absorbed into your bloodstream. Chewing your food is beneficial for the same reason.

Maximize Your Juice Potential

Getting the most out of your precious juice elixirs and cocktails has a lot to do with timing. When you drink fresh-squeezed juices on an empty stomach, your body's attention is devoted to the digestion and absorption of vital nutrients into your bloodstream. If whole foods, which take longer to digest, are present in your stomach, the absorption and assimilation of the juice is slowed down. Try separating your juice intake from your ingestion of whole foods. Fresh fruits act as intestinal cleansers, and vegetables provide the vitamins and minerals important to good nutrition. Drinking fresh fruit juice first thing in the morning cleanses the stomach, colon and digestive tract. Raw vegetable juice taken before your meal, at mid-afternoon breaks or as a nightcap will keep your energy levels up, your cravings in check and your body hydrated with nourishing fluids.

Juice Fasting

Detox, short for detoxification, is the removal of potentially toxic substances from the body. In particular, juice fasting is an excellent way of removing environmental and dietary toxins from the body for general health. Juice fasting gives your body a rest from the multi-faceted chore of digestion, assimilation and elimination. Fresh fruit and vegetable juice fasting is an effective way to divert your body's energy inward to the demanding job of cleansing and detoxifying your colon, intestinal tract, organs and blood, while replenishing its store of vitamins and minerals. The length of fast can run from one to twelve days, depending on your experience and the demands of your life and work. I have trouble fasting while I'm working, so I plan my juice fasting for holidays and days off, when I'm more relaxed.

It is common to feel chilled to the bone when fasting as your body detoxifies and cleanses, so choosing the warmer months, with the added sunshine, is a good idea. A daily hot Epsom salt bath will relax your muscles and help draw out the impurities in your body when you are feeling cold.

Spring is the season for renewal and growth. This is my favourite time of the year for an annual fast. Consistency and regularity are more important than how long you fast. In the same way your body gets used to regular exercise, and even craves it, it will also come to anticipate the regimen of a fast the same day each week, or three days at the end of each month, or one week every year.

The preparation for a typical juice fast can begin up to seven days before the start of the fast itself. Although it is normal to initially experience hunger, light-headedness and some nausea during a juice fast, it will be much worse if you don't ease your body into it gradually and try going cold turkey. This involves reducing or eliminating alcohol, nicotine, caffeine, sugar, dairy, wheat, meat, fish and eggs from your diet. Ease up on breads, pastas, packaged and fried foods. Increase your intake of fresh, easy-to-digest foods such as fruits, salads, brown rice, beans and soy products. Choose organic whenever possible and if not, then be sure to wash unpeeled produce with a non-toxic cleaner, usually available at health food stores.

Between 32 and 64 ounces of juice is usually recommended per day. The juice is sipped throughout the day. Typical fruits and vegetables include celery, carrot, kale, cucumber, apple, pineapple, pear, cranberry, spinach, beet, lemon, parsley and ginger. Green vegetables and sprouts, high in chlorophyll, are especially beneficial during a juice fast. Chlorophyll is a powerful detoxifier and blood builder. Green vegetables and sprouts, when juiced, actually become sweeter. Citrus foods should be kept to a minimum due to their high levels of acidity.

Recently, it has been discovered that grapefruit juice should not be used during a juice fast, especially while taking prescription drugs. A compound in grapefruit can increase the effect of prescription drugs in a person's body. For something warm, try making a large batch of vegetable broth, adding herbs and spices, at the start of your fast and enjoy a bowl for lunch or dinner each day. A savory bowl of broth can feel like a gourmet four-course meal when you are fasting.

At least 6 glasses of room-temperature, filtered water per day is also recommended. Despite drinking gallons of juice, you still need to drink pure water. Staying hydrated will help your body flush the toxins out of your system faster. I often feel that the glow I get from fasting is in part because I've been drinking more water.

When you are ready to end your fast, you should return gradually to solid foods in small frequent portions. As you introduce solid food back into your diet, be sure to take the time to chew food well so it is more easily digested. Eating again after a fast can be very exciting, but try not to overeat and take it slow. To get the most out of your efforts, reverse the preparation stage at the start of your fast and eat this way for up to seven days after your fast as well. This is your opportunity to let go of any bad habits for a while and to let your body return to a reinvigorated state of balance and health.

Hot Juice

Several years ago I discovered that if I heated certain juices, the flavour and potency of some of the ingredients was heightened. Heating ingredients like pineapple, pear, apple, ginger, garlic, lemon or cayenne enhances their active qualities: the cayenne gets hotter, the pineapple sweeter, the ginger spicier and the garlic sharper. Thus, the Lung Lover, Flu Fighter, Hot Apple Pie, Deep Immune and Singer's Saving Grace were born. When heating juice in a saucepan, be sure never to bring it to a boil in order to preserve the nutrients as much as possible. Stir it frequently and remove it when it's warm and ready for sipping. You can also use the steamer on a cappuccino machine for heating juice. It's faster.

Energy, Immune and Wheatgrass Elixirs

Energy, Immune and Wheatgrass Elixirs are juice concoctions combined with nutritional power boosts designed to provide particular benefits.

Fruit smoothies, vegetable cocktails and other combinations provide a delicious liquid backdrop that enhances the benefits and effects of added herbal tinctures, superfood supplements, protein powders and wheatgrass.

Energy Elixirs

Super Energy Cocktail

I get foggy and a little slow every day around 3 p.m. Since coffee makes me anxious, I created the Super Energy Cocktail to clear my head and wake me up. This is a sweet, light and hydrating cocktail that carries the revitalizing nutrients of the superfood supplement to the body's cells for rapid absorption and assimilation. The result is an energy boost that is gentle and uplifting—with no crash landings.

Ingredients

1/2 inch	ginger root
4 slices	pineapple
3 oz.	filtered water
1/2	cucumber
2 medium	red apples
1 tbsp.	Greens+ (see p. 196)

Method

Juice the ginger first. Follow with the pineapple slices, adding a bit of filtered water to flush the juice through. Juice the cucumber, and last, the apples. Stir in the Greens+. Pour into a tall glass. For a smoother cocktail, use a blender to mix in the Greens+.

Liquid Lunch Box Energy Elixir

This is a drink for those of us who don't have time to eat but need the fuel and nourishment to get through the day at work, the gym or a yoga class. This drink is best served cold.

Ingredients

2 medium	yellow pears
3 medium	red apples
1	banana, peeled
1	kiwi, peeled
1 tbsp.	Spirutein (see p. 197)

Method

Juice the pears first. Follow with the apples. Transfer mixture to the blender and add the banana. Start on a low setting while you add the kiwi and Spirutein powder. Switch to a higher setting and blend for about a minute. Pour into a tall glass.

Supersonic Energy Elixir New!

If you have loved the Lust for Life for a long time and are ready for a new love, then try this. Equally delicious, we have taken the banana and kiwi out and added more berries for greater antioxidant appeal.

Ingredients

8 oz.	**bottled mango juice**
2 tbsp.	**blueberries (fresh or frozen)**
6	**strawberries (fresh or frozen)**
2 tbsp.	**raspberries (fresh or frozen)**
1 vial	**panax ginseng (see p. 200)**

Method

Place the mango juice and berries in the blender. Start on a low setting and switch to a higher setting for about a minute. Pour into a tall glass. Swirl in the ginseng.

Bionic Brain Tonic Energy Elixir

This drink was actor Joseph Fiennes' favourite combination. He'd been coming in to drink it almost daily while he was in town shooting a film. When he came in one day and ordered one, I had just seen Shakespeare in Love. *I got so flustered I put all the wrong ingredients in his drink. That was the last time we ever saw him. How embarrassing!*

Ingredients

3 medium	red apples
1	banana, peeled
4 oz.	coconut milk
6	strawberries (fresh or frozen)
1 vial	panax ginseng (see p. 200)
1 vial	gingko biloba (see p. 199)

Method

Juice the apples first. Transfer juice to the blender and add the banana and coconut milk. Start on a low setting while you add the strawberries. Switch to a higher setting and blend for about a minute. Drop in the ginseng and gingko. Pour into a tall glass.

Einstein's Theory Energy Elixir

Did you know that Albert Einstein was a vegetarian? Smart man. Eric Clapton ordered this combination at the first Queen Street location. Gingko biloba is a favourite among musicians, especially drummers, concerned about their hearing. Gingko increases circulation of blood to the brain and protects your eardrums from the dangers of tinnitus. An increased flow of blood to the brain also sharpens memory and mental clarity.

Ingredients

3 medium	yellow or green pears
2	oranges
1	banana, peeled
1 vial	gingko biloba (see p. 199)

Method

Juice the pears first. Follow with the oranges. Transfer the pear and orange juice to the blender, and add the banana. Start on a low setting. Switch to a higher setting and blend for about one minute. Swirl in the gingko. Pour into a tall glass.

Lust for Life Energy Elixir

Named after the Iggy Pop song at a time when I was feeling especially positive and excited about my life and future, this mixture has become our best-selling energy elixir. The blueberries make this drink a gorgeous blue-purple colour.

Ingredients

8 oz.	bottled mango juice
1	banana, peeled
1	kiwi, peeled
2 tbsp.	blueberries (fresh or frozen)
1 vial	panax ginseng (see p. 200)

Method

Put the mango juice and banana in the blender. Start on a low setting while you add the kiwi and blueberries. Switch to a higher setting and blend for about a minute. Pour into a tall glass. Swirl in the ginseng.

100 Metre Dash Energy Elixir

This is considered the hard-core juice-lover's cocktail. The lemon lightens up this elixir to make drinking your green vegetables a little easier. I like to add a shake of cayenne pepper to give the drink a bit of zip. Green vegetable juice is packed with live enzymes, chlorophyll, vitamins and minerals. Its alkaline properties help neutralize acidity and rebalance your body chemistry to give you optimum digestion and more energy. Never mind the 100 metre dash—you will want to run a marathon after drinking one of these.

Ingredients

1 handful	spinach
10 stalks	parsley
1/2	lemon, peeled
1	large cucumber
6 stalks	celery
1 tbsp.	Greens+ (see p. 196)

Method

Juice the spinach and parsley first. Follow with the lemon and cucumber. Finish with the celery. Stir in the Greens+. Pour into a tall glass.

Woman's Roar Energy Elixir

This is one of my favourites when I'm feeling premenstrual. The cucumber reduces water retention, the ginger soothes the stomach, the beet cleanses and enriches the blood and finally, the Greens+ picks me up and makes me wanna ROAR!

Ingredients

1/2 inch	ginger root
1/2	beet, scrubbed
2	red apples
1	cucumber
1 tbsp.	Greens+ (see p. 196)

Method

Juice the ginger first. Follow with the beet and apple. Flush through with the cucumber. Stir in the Greens+. Pour into a tall glass.

Immune Elixirs

Immune Boost Elixir

Willem Dafoe, the actor, enjoyed this combination after his ashtanga yoga class when he was in Toronto one spring. When this elixir starts getting ordered a lot, it usually means there's a flu or cold bug going around. Customers will often come in complaining of the same symptoms. That's when we start making extra for ourselves, just to be safe.

Ingredients

1/2 inch	ginger root
1 small	beet, scrubbed
2 medium	red apples
2 medium	carrots
1/2 tsp.	vitamin C powder (see p. 197)
20 drops	echinacea (see p. 199)

Method

Juice the ginger first. Follow with the beet and apples. Juice the carrots last. Stir in the vitamin C powder. Drop in the echinacea tincture. Pour into a tall glass.

Full Court Press Immune Elixir

Full court press is a basketball term. All the players on a team steamroll down the court to try to overwhelm the opponents and save the game. This is my approach when I feel a virus trying to invade my body. I pull out the heavy artillery and declare war on the invaders. This means drinking lots of fluids, juice, herbal tinctures and teas. I'm usually back on my feet in a day or two.

Ingredients

1/2 inch	ginger root
1/2	lemon, peeled
2 medium	yellow pears
3 medium	red apples
20 drops	echinacea (see p. 199)
20 drops	goldenseal (see p. 200)

Method

Juice the ginger first. Follow with the lemon, pears and apples. Drop in the echinacea and goldenseal. Pour into a tall glass. For a warm cocktail, heat juice gently in a saucepan. To preserve the nutrients, be careful not to bring it to a boil. Pour into a mug and drop in the tinctures.

Liver Flush Immune Elixir

Formerly called Bukowski's Liver Flush after the prolific poet and devout alcoholic Charles Bukowski, this combination is spicy, sweet and intense. You can gradually increase the amount of beet juice in this recipe as you become accustomed to its detoxifying effect on your body. Beet juice has powerful cleansing benefits to the liver, kidneys and blood. Be sure to drink lots of water throughout the day.

Ingredients

1/2 inch	ginger root
2 medium	beets, scrubbed
1/2	lemon, peeled
2 large	pink grapefruits
2 shakes	cayenne pepper
20 drops	milk thistle (see p. 200)

Method

Juice the ginger first. Follow with the beets and lemon. Finish with the grapefruit. Stir in the cayenne pepper. Drop in the milk thistle. Pour into a tall glass.

Winter Sunshine Immune Elixir

This fruit-based high "C" elixir was developed for those customers looking to avoid, at all costs, a vegetable-based immune boost. Guaranteed to put a smile on your face.

Ingredients

4 slices	pineapple
3 oz.	filtered water
2	oranges, peeled
1	banana, peeled
1/2	kiwi, peeled
1/2 tsp.	vitamin C powder (see p. 197)
1 vial	royal jelly (see p. 200)

Method

Juice the pineapple first. Flush through with filtered water. Follow with the oranges. In the blender, place the pineapple and orange juice with the banana. Start on a low setting while you add the kiwi and vitamin C. Switch to a higher setting and blend for about a minute. Swirl in the royal jelly. Pour into a tall glass.

Iron Maiden Immune Elixir

This juice is designed for women who tend to get low in iron and feel otherwise depleted after that special time of the month. Thinking I was making a funny pun, I named it after the rock band. Then they actually came into our Queen Street Market location and ordered it during a live interview.

Ingredients

1 handful	spinach
1 small	beet, scrubbed
4	medium carrots
1 tsp.	spirulina (see p. 196)

Method

Juice the spinach first. Follow with the beet. Finish with the carrots. Transfer juice to a blender, and add the spirulina while the juice is spinning on a low setting. A blender is essential to mix in the powder because it is so fine and gets sticky when wet. Pour into a tall glass.

Deep Immune Elixir (Hot)

Sweet and spicy, this exotic drink warms my bones and keeps the fire going in my body through the winter. For less sweetness, reduce the number of dates. For more spiciness, increase the amount of ginger. The banana adds thickness but is not essential.

Ingredients

6	dates, soaked in hot water
1/2 inch	ginger root
4 medium	red apples
1	lemon, peeled
1/2	banana, peeled
1 tbsp.	chywanprash (see p. 196)

Method

Soak the dates in hot water for 15 minutes. In the meantime, juice the ginger. Follow with the apples and lemon. Put the ginger, apple and lemon juice in the blender with the banana. Start on a low setting while you add the soaked dates and chywanprash paste. Blend for about 2 minutes. Heat gently in a saucepan until juice is nice and warm. Do not boil. Pour into a mug. Sip slowly.

Lung Lover Immune Elixir Hot

This recipe was created in response to our customers' requests for relief from chest colds, flu-like symptoms and chills. The combination of warm ginger root and cayenne pepper gets the blood circulating and the body sweating, while you're innocently enjoying the sweet flavour of cooked apples.

Ingredients

1/2 inch	ginger root
1/2	lemon, peeled
4 medium	red apples
1 shake	cayenne pepper
10 drops	licorice root (see p. 200)
10 drops	osha root (see p. 200)
10 drops	echinacea (see p. 199)

Method

Juice the ginger first. Follow with the lemon and the apples. Shake in the cayenne pepper. Heat gently in a saucepan until juice is nice and warm. Do not boil. Drop in the tinctures. Pour into a mug. Sip slowly.

Singer's Saving Grace Immune Elixir Hot

Many of our city's gifted singers swear by this concoction. Sipping one of these before or after a performance soothes the voice and throat. Pineapple juice and ginger root both have mild anti-histaminic and anti-inflammatory properties. Licorice root is also an effective adrenal gland support.

Ingredients

1/2 inch	ginger root
2 medium	yellow or green pears
6 slices	pineapple
3 oz.	filtered water
1 shake	cloves
1 vial	royal jelly (see p. 200)
20 drops	licorice root (see p. 200)

Method

Juice the ginger first. Follow with the pears and pineapple. Pour in the filtered water to flush the juice through. Shake in the cloves. Heat gently in a saucepan until juice is nice and warm. Do not boil. Drop in the royal jelly and licorice root. Pour into a mug and sip slowly.

Wheatgrass Elixirs

Someone once remarked to me that wheatgrass tastes like you mowed the front lawn with your mouth. Wheatgrass is very sweet yet green, like an unripe banana. It's an acquired taste. I love the immediate jolt of energy that seems to last for the whole day, but I do have a hard time drinking it straight up. Steve Tyler of Aerosmith has been known to order 10 ounces of fresh-pressed wheatgrass from us before a show when he's in town. Asked in an interview what he does for kicks now that he is drug-free, he replied that he mainlines wheatgrass.

If you don't have a manual or electric wheatgrass juicer, you can buy your wheatgrass frozen from the health food store in convenient 1-ounce shots. Drop a 1-ounce frozen cube of wheatgrass into your juice and let thaw for 5 minutes before drinking.

Singing Grasshopper Wheatgrass Elixir

While searching for painless new ways to take my wheatgrass shots, I discovered that peppermint and wheatgrass make a heavenly combination. The taste of the peppermint masks the wheatgrass nicely and leaves your mouth feeling fresh and clean. Pure oil of peppermint has anti-microbial properties. These properties enhance the actions of the immune and digestive systems. It is available in most health food stores and specialty food stores.

Ingredients

8 oz.	bottled mango juice
1	banana, peeled
1 tsp.	unpasteurized honey
10 drops	pure oil of peppermint
1 oz.	wheatgrass juice (see p. 198)

Method

Place the mango juice, banana and honey in the blender. Start on a low setting and switch to a higher setting for about a minute. Pour into a tall glass. Drop the peppermint and wheatgrass into the glass.

Strawberry Fields Wheatgrass Elixir

This is a great way to drink wheatgrass if you are new at this. Drinking the wheatgrass in a smoothie allows your body to metabolize and absorb it at a slower pace while giving you time to get used to the taste. Once you've mastered this, you can try drinking wheatgrass alone and chasing it with a liquid of your choice.

Ingredients

6 slices	pineapple
3 oz.	filtered water
1	banana, peeled
6	strawberries (fresh or frozen)
1 oz.	wheatgrass juice (see p. 198)

Method

Juice the pineapple first. Add the filtered water to flush the juice through. Put the pineapple juice in the blender with the banana. Start on a low setting while you add the strawberries. Pour into a tall glass. Drop the wheatgrass into the glass.

Liquid Oxygen Wheatgrass Elixir

This juice is a vibrant lime-green colour that reminds me of the first exciting days of spring.

Ingredients

4 slices	pineapple
3 oz.	filtered water
2	oranges
1	banana, peeled
1 oz.	wheatgrass juice (see p. 198)

Method

Juice the pineapple. Add the filtered water to flush the juice through. Follow with the oranges. Transfer mixture to the blender and add the banana. Start on a low setting and switch to a higher setting for about a minute. Pour into a tall glass. Drop the wheatgrass into the glass.

Hangover Helper Wheatgrass Elixir

Although this combination is a Martian-like green colour, the dominant flavour is fruity, sweet and refreshing. The chlorophyll in the wheatgrass oxygenates the blood, detoxifies the organs and gives the cells a boost of potent energy. The spirulina replenishes the body's store of nutrients, especially the B vitamins, which are depleted by the effects of stress and alcohol. It's the magic antidote to your wayward habits.

Ingredients

3	oranges
1	banana, peeled
1 tbsp.	spirulina (see p. 196)
1 oz.	wheatgrass juice (see p. 198)

Method

Juice the oranges first. Transfer the orange juice to the blender and add the banana. Start on a low setting while you add the spirulina—drop the spirulina in once the liquid is spinning so it won't stick to the sides. Pour into a tall glass. Drop the wheatgrass into the glass.

Super Power Shakes

Our Super Power Shakes are dairy-free milkshakes blended with a variety of supplements or boosts. We use organic vanilla soymilk and banana as a base from which to create thick, creamy, fruity and delicious shakes.

Coconut milk, fresh berries and peaches, tropical fruit juices, oats, maple syrup, honey, dates, nut butters and exotic spices are added to make combinations that are filling and satisfying. To these we add nutritional boosts such as wheat germ, spirulina, royal jelly or a protein powder. The possibilities can be endless once you get to know the basic formula. Rice milk, almond milk or oat milk are delicious substitutes for soymilk.

ZenMatcha Power Shake New!

Matcha green tea powder is approximately 10 times stronger than a regular cup of brewed green tea, with a high concentration of antioxidants. It has a delicate flavour that combines very nicely with the pineapple and cinnamon. The energy you get from the matcha is gradual and prolonged with no sudden highs or lows. I find I am not hungry for several hours after I have had this shake.

Ingredients

4 slices	pineapple
3 oz.	filtered water
1	banana, peeled
6 oz.	vanilla soymilk
1 shake	cinnamon
1 tbsp.	matcha green tea powder (see p. 197)

Method

Juice the pineapple. Add filtered water to flush the juice through. Place the pineapple, banana, soymilk, cinnamon and matcha green tea powder in the blender. Start on a low setting and switch to a higher setting for about a minute. Pour into a tall glass.

Ripped Power Shake New!

This shake makes no apologies about being high in carbohydrates. Along with the high-protein content, it is designed to give you the fuel you need to start your workout or as a post-workout recovery meal in a glass. It also makes for a delicious and filling breakfast smoothie as you run out the door. Whoever thought that blending your granola was a good idea? Well, try it and see how good it can be.

Ingredients

2 tbsp.	Fresh Granola (see p. 114)
1	banana, peeled
8 oz.	vanilla rice milk
1 shake	cinnamon
1 tbsp.	Spirutein (see p. 197)

Method

Place the granola, banana, rice milk and cinnamon in the blender. Start on a low setting while you add the protein powder and switch to a higher setting for about a minute. Pour into a tall glass.

Omega Power Shake New!

Did you know that the pomegranate is one of the first domesticated crops in recorded history? Today, the pomegranate is acclaimed for its health benefits, in particular, for its disease-fighting antioxidant potential. What are antioxidants? Simply put, antioxidants protect our bodies from harmful molecules we are exposed to every day. Antioxidants are ingested primarily as components of fruits and vegetables. You will find natural unsweetened pomegranate juice in most health food stores and specialty food stores. I have added the soymilk and banana to offset the mild tartness of the pomegranate and cranberries.

Ingredients

8 oz.	bottled pomegranate juice
2 tbsp.	blueberries (fresh or frozen)
2 tbsp.	pitted cranberries (fresh or frozen)
1	banana, peeled
4 oz.	vanilla soymilk

Method

Place the pomegranate juice, berries, banana and soymilk in the blender. Start on a low setting and switch to a higher setting for about a minute. Pour into a tall glass.

Liquid Yoga Power Shake (New!)

This is a great example of a wonderful supplement looking for a home. I created the Liquid Yoga as a great-tasting backdrop to the Hemp, Sprouted Flax and Maca Protein. The brand we use is called Ruth's, but you can also find other kinds of good-quality vegan protein powders at many health food stores these days.

Ingredients

2 tbsp.	raspberries (fresh or frozen)
8 oz.	vanilla rice milk
1	banana, peeled
1 tbsp.	Hemp, Sprouted Flax and Maca Protein (see p. 197)

Method

Place the raspberries, banana, rice milk and protein in the blender. Start on a low setting and switch to a higher setting for about a minute. Pour into a tall glass.

Super Protein Power Shake

This is one of our original recipes from the Queen Street Market days. This shake is bright green, creamy, filling and yummy. In addition to its high protein content, it contains spirulina, a blue-green algae that provides a concentrated source of beta-carotene and B vitamins, especially B12.

Ingredients

12 oz.	vanilla soymilk
1	banana, peeled
1 tbsp.	spirulina (see p. 196)

Method

Put the soymilk and banana in the blender. Start the blender on a low setting while you add the spirulina powder. Switch to a higher setting and blend for about a minute. Pour into a tall glass.

Blueberry Thrills Power Shake

The Super Protein Power Shake is the base for this combination (see page 161). Add blueberries and you get the antioxidant benefits, too!

Ingredients

12 oz.	vanilla soymilk
1	banana, peeled
2 tbsp.	blueberries (fresh or frozen)
1 tbsp.	spirulina (see p. 196)

Aphrodisiac Power Shake

Mangos, coconut and nutmeg are very sexy fruits and spices. The scent, colour, texture and taste of these ingredients are reputed to have aphrodisiac effects, a belief held by many men and women in the Caribbean islands. I've included the royal jelly to give your body the energy and stamina it will likely need once you've drunk this potion.

Ingredients

4 oz.	bottled mango juice
4 oz.	vanilla soymilk
1	banana, peeled
4 oz.	coconut milk
1 shake	nutmeg
1 vial	royal jelly (see p. 200)

Method

Put the mango juice, soymilk and banana in the blender. Start the blender on a low setting while you add the coconut milk and nutmeg. Switch to a higher setting and blend for about 2 minutes. Pour into a tall glass. Swirl the royal jelly into the shake.

Date Almond Power Shake

The Date Almond Power Shake makes for a delicious dessert drink. The almond butter has a delicate nutty flavour that is enhanced even more by the exotic sweetness of the dates. This drink also doubles as a super protein power shake. Bodybuilders looking for extra calories and complex carbohydrates can enjoy this all-natural shake.

Ingredients

4	dates, soaked in hot water
6 oz.	vanilla soymilk
1	banana, peeled
1 tbsp.	almond butter
1 tsp.	maple syrup
1 shake	cinnamon

Method

Soak the dates in hot water for 5 minutes. Put the soymilk, soaked dates and banana in the blender. Start the blender on a low setting while you add the almond butter, maple syrup and cinnamon. Switch to a higher setting and blend for about 2 minutes. Pour into a tall glass.

Espresso Shakes

Espresso shakes are a great way to get a powerful boost of fuel while also drinking in a dose of good nutrition. Making your own shake with wholesome ingredients like banana, almond butter, maple syrup or an enriched low-fat milk means you can avoid the high-fat coffee drinks out there. Espresso shakes taste best really cold so be sure to use ice when blending. Or, for added thickness, you can freeze your peeled bananas ahead of time and use instead of ice. At Fresh, we offer a selection of organic milks to go in your coffee. Tasty natural sweeteners can include maple syrup, honey, stevia or agave nectar. Freshly ground coffee is always preferable as the oils in coffee beans easily go rancid once ground and can make your coffee bitter.

Today, the definition of what makes a good cup of coffee is broadening to include the quality of life and the quality of the natural environment where our coffees are grown. At Fresh, we use certified fair trade, organic shade grown espresso or coffee beans. It's a term you are probably familiar with, but what does it really mean?

It's fairly simple. Buying fair trade coffee guarantees that the community-based growers are getting a fair deal. The political and moral issue of coffee involves large plantations in Latin America where profits stay in the hands of a few corporate land owners. Fair Trade certification ensures that the farmers who grow the coffee are compensated fairly, allowing the profits from their harvests to be reinvested in their own communities. The irony is that the certification fee is more than many of these farmers can afford even if they are already farming organically. There is now a growing movement to use a portion of the proceeds to lend the farmers the funds to get started.

Organic and shade grown certification ensures that coffee is preserving, not destroying, the natural environment where it is grown. No chemicals, no pesticides, no clear-cutting: coffee is grown under the forest canopy by farmers committed to the quality of their crop.

Rocket Fuel Espresso Shake

Despite repeated experiences confirming that I shouldn't drink coffee because it makes me completely neurotic, I still love the aroma, taste and ritual of it. I find this delicious shake hard to resist. It's one of the originals.

Ingredients

1 dbl. shot	espresso or brewed coffee
6 oz.	vanilla soymilk
1	banana, peeled
1 tsp.	maple syrup
1 shake	cinnamon
6	ice cubes

Method

Make the shot of espresso or coffee first. Place the soymilk and banana in the blender. Start the blender on a low setting while you add the espresso, maple syrup, cinnamon and ice. Switch to a higher setting and blend for about 2 minutes. Pour into a tall glass.

Mocha Mint Espresso Shake

This new shake doubles as a peppermint chocolate latte if served warm. Did you know that dark cocoa possesses the nutrient phenylethylamine, a natural amphetamine that induces euphoria? Dark cocoa also contains the four essential nutrients: iron, calcium, potassium and magnesium. The yoga students often order this one before class. Is that cheating?

Ingredients

1 dbl. shot	espresso or brewed coffee
6 oz.	vanilla soymilk
1 tbsp.	dark cocoa powder
10 drops	pure oil of peppermint
1 tsp.	raw sugar
6	ice cubes

Method

Make the shot of espresso or coffee first. Place the soymilk in the blender. Start the blender on a low setting while you add the espresso, dark cocoa, peppermint, raw sugar and ice. Switch to a higher setting and blend for about 2 minutes. Pour into a tall glass.

Almond Java Espresso Shake New!

This is our version of a healthy coffee shake. Get your protein, calcium and caffeine fix right here.

Ingredients

1 dbl. shot	espresso or brewed coffee
6 oz.	vanilla soymilk
1 tbsp.	almond butter
1	banana, peeled
1 tsp.	maple syrup
6	ice cubes

Method

Make the shot of espresso or coffee first. Place the soymilk, almond butter and banana in the blender. Start the blender on a low setting while you add the espresso, maple syrup and ice. Switch to a higher setting and blend for about 2 minutes. Pour into a tall glass.

Vanilla Chip Espresso Shake New!

I created this healthier combination for those hooked on the Starbucks Java Chip version. I didn't anticipate that the chocolate chips would be like candy for the bartenders. I can see why: I find it hard to resist grabbing a scoop when I am back there.

Ingredients

1 dbl. shot	espresso or coffee
6 oz.	vanilla soymilk
1 tbsp.	unsweetened dark chocolate chips
20 drops	pure vanilla extract
1 tsp.	raw sugar
1 shake	cinnamon
6	ice cubes

Method

Make the shot of espresso or coffee first. Place the soymilk, dark chocolate chips, vanilla extract, raw sugar, cinnamon and ice in the blender. Start the blender on a low setting; switch to a higher setting and blend for about 2 minutes. Pour into a tall glass.

> First Kiss Smoothie   177

Fresh Fruit Smoothies

Fresh smoothies are heavenly combinations of fruit juice blended with fresh whole fruit. They are the supreme fuel to start your body's engine each day. Smoothies fill you up without slowing you down. You will see that our low-fat smoothies do not need dairy, yogurt or sweeteners to make them thick, sweet and satisfying. Bananas are a great non-dairy thickener for smoothies and are an ideal energy food, rich in potassium and high in fruit sugars. The riper they are, the sweeter the smoothie will be. It's simple to make a smoothie. Fresh-squeezed juices such as orange, mango, pineapple, apple, grapefruit or pear are blended with soft fruits such as banana, strawberries, blueberries, kiwi or peach.

Antioxidant Smoothie (New!)

This slightly tart smoothie is a nice change from our mostly sweet-tasting selection. You can always add soymilk if you would like to sweeten it up a wee bit. After much experimentation I have found that pomegranate juice and blueberries complement each other best for flavour in a smoothie. Neither dominates.

Ingredients

8 oz.	bottled pomegranate juice
1	banana, peeled
2 tbsp.	blueberries (fresh or frozen)

Method

Place the pomegranate juice and banana in the blender. Start on a low setting while you add the blueberries. Switch to a higher setting for about a minute. Pour into a tall glass.

Susur Smoothie (New!)

Our entire staff is addicted to this dazzling smoothie that is named after internationally acclaimed chef Susur Lee. Susur created this lovely combination and always requests it when he comes in for a juice.

Ingredients

1	small beet, scrubbed
3	red apples
2 tbsp.	raspberries (fresh or frozen)
6	ice cubes

Method

Juice the beet first. Follow with the apple. Place in a blender with the raspberries and ice. Start on a low setting and switch to a higher setting for about a minute. Pour into a tall glass.

Elvis Smoothie

When naming smoothies, sometimes I go for the obvious connection. This smoothie tastes just like a fabulous peanut butter, banana and jelly sandwich. This leads us to Elvis Presley, who was famous for eating them all day long.

Ingredients

4	red apples
1 tbsp.	natural peanut butter
1	banana, peeled

Method

Juice the apples first. Place in the blender with the peanut butter and banana. Start on a low setting and switch to a higher setting for about a minute. Pour into a tall glass.

Dragonfly Smoothie (New!)

Kids love this smoothie. It's simple, sweet and a pretty pink colour.

Ingredients

4	red apples
2 tbsp.	raspberries (fresh or frozen)
1	banana, peeled

Method

Juice the apples first. Place in the blender with the raspberries and banana. Start on a low setting and switch to a higher setting for about a minute. Pour into a tall glass.

First Kiss Smoothie

I love that exhilarating first kiss that is so full of discovery and promise. Close your eyes when you have this smoothie and you might get something close to that sensation. Most people are surprised to hear that strawberries are higher in vitamin C and lower in fruit sugars than oranges. This makes them a better choice when you have a cold and should be avoiding sugars, which suppress the immune system.

Ingredients

6 slices	pineapple
3 oz.	filtered water
1	banana, peeled
6	strawberries (fresh or frozen)

Method

Juice the pineapple. Add filtered water to flush the juice through. Put the pineapple juice and banana in the blender. Start on a low setting while you add the strawberries. Switch to a higher setting for about a minute. Pour into a tall glass.

Blue Lagoon Smoothie

When people order this one, I can tell they are dreaming of an exotic holiday and hoping this smoothie will bring them one air mile closer to that dream.

Ingredients

8 oz.	bottled mango juice
1	banana, peeled
2 tbsp.	blueberries (fresh or frozen)

Method

Put the mango juice and banana in the blender. Start on a low setting while you add the blueberries. Switch to a higher setting for about a minute. Pour into a tall glass.

Rise and Shine Smoothie

Grapefruit juice, when taken first thing in the morning, initiates the cleansing of the intestinal tract and stimulates regular bowel movements. The red-fleshed grapefruit is sweeter and less acidic than white grapefruit. In this instance, it's good to include some of the white pith surrounding the flesh in your juice because it supplies the bioflavanoids that help the body to retain and use vitamin C, which grapefruit has in abundance.

Ingredients

2	pink grapefruits
2	oranges
6	strawberries (fresh or frozen)

Method

Juice the grapefruit and oranges. Put the grapefruit and orange juice in the blender. Start on a low setting while you add the strawberries. Switch to a higher setting for about a minute. Pour into a tall glass.

Pink Flamingo Smoothie

Watermelon juice is a natural diuretic that is sweet and refreshing. It's low in calories and loaded with digestive enzymes, and its high water content helps flush the bladder and kidneys of toxins and excess fluids. This pretty pink smoothie is absolutely captivating and mouthwateringly delicious.

Ingredients

6 slices	watermelon
1	banana, peeled
6	strawberries (fresh or frozen)

Method

You can run the watermelon slices through the juicer or purée them with the rest of the ingredients in the blender. Put the watermelon and banana in the blender. Start on a low setting while you add the strawberries. Switch to a higher setting for about a minute. Pour into a tall glass.

Zest for Life Smoothie

This smoothie is invigorating. One medium-sized orange contains almost twice the recommended daily allowance of vitamin C, while the pith (the white stuff that surrounds the flesh of the orange) supplies the bioflavanoids needed to absorb it. Pineapple juice is very high in the elusive digestive enzyme bromelain, which helps the stomach to balance and neutralize fluids that are too acidic or too alkaline. It is also high in vitamin C, potassium and natural fruit acids. Kiwi adds more punch to this smoothie with its tartness and abundant vitamin C content.

Ingredients

4 slices	pineapple
3 oz.	filtered water
2	oranges
1	kiwi, peeled

Method

Juice the pineapple. Add filtered water to flush the juice through. Follow with the oranges. Put the juice in the blender with the kiwi. Start on a low setting. Switch to a higher setting for about a minute. Pour into a tall glass.

Breathless Smoothie

Tropical mango juice is often referred to as the "nectar of the gods." Rich in beta-carotene and vitamin C, mangos are fragrant, with a silky texture and peachy flavour. Because mangos are too thick and fleshy to juice or drink on their own, mango juice is generally bottled with a neutral base like white grape juice.

Ingredients

8 oz.	bottled mango juice
1	banana, peeled
6	strawberries (fresh or frozen)

Method

Put the mango juice and banana in the blender. Start on a low setting while you add the strawberries. Switch to a higher setting and blend for about a minute. Pour into a tall glass.

Negril Beach Smoothie

Negril Beach in Jamaica is a tropical paradise. This smoothie is what I imagine myself sipping on the beach under a palm tree. Bananas are an ideal energy food, rich in potassium and high in fruit sugars. They are also a great non-dairy thickener for smoothies. The riper they are, the sweeter the smoothie will be. Really ripe bananas, peeled and frozen, can be saved and used later to make super-thick and creamy smoothies.

Ingredients

6 oz.	bottled mango juice
1	banana, peeled
4 oz.	coconut milk
	ice (optional)

Method

Place the mango juice and banana in the blender. Start on a low setting, then add the coconut milk and ice (optional). Switch to a higher setting for about a minute. Pour into a tall glass.

Sunsplash Smoothie

The kiwi gives this smoothie a less sweet, more tangy flavour. Kiwi paired with oranges gives this smoothie a real punch of vitamin C.

Ingredients

3	oranges, peeled
1	banana, peeled
1	kiwi, peeled
	ice (optional)

Method

Run the oranges through the juicer. Place the juice in the blender with the banana. Start on a low setting while you add the kiwi and ice (optional). Switch to a higher setting for about a minute. Pour into a tall glass.

Empress Smoothie

This simple, refreshing smoothie is great for early mornings and a good base for exciting ingredients like raspberries or blackberries.

Ingredients

4 slices	pineapple
3 oz.	filtered water
2	oranges, peeled
1	banana, peeled
	ice (optional)

Method

Juice the pineapple. Run a little filtered water to flush the juice through. Follow with the oranges. Place the juice in the blender with the banana. Start on a low setting while you add ice (optional). Switch to a higher setting for about a minute. Pour into a tall glass.

Hot Apple Pie Smoothie

This is a great winter drink. Apple juice, when heated, takes on the same homey flavour as baked apples, and the cooked banana becomes sweet and thick like maple syrup. The ginger and lemon add a little spice to the mix. You can leave out the banana and increase the lemon and ginger for a soothing cold buster.

Ingredients

1/2 inch	ginger root
1/2	lemon, peeled
4 medium	red apples
1	banana, peeled
1 shake	cinnamon

Method

Juice the ginger and lemon. Follow with the apples. Put the juice in the blender with the banana. Start on a low setting while you shake in the cinnamon. Switch to a higher setting for about a minute. Heat gently in a saucepan until juice is nice and warm. Stir. Do not bring to a boil. Pour into a large mug. If you don't have a juicer, skip the ginger and use apple cider with a squeeze of lemon; mix all ingredients in a blender. Pour into a tall glass.

Vegetable Cocktails

Today, conventional high-yield farming practices result in produce being grown in soil depleted of nutrients, while stress and a busy lifestyle further inhibit our ability to get what we need out of our food. A healthy diet is no longer enough to ensure we are getting the necessary nutrients our bodies crave. In just one glass, we can get more fresh vegetables than we have time to prepare.

Drinking your vegetables is always more fun than eating them. Juicing vegetables unlocks their high concentration of nutrients from the fibre and allows your body easy and quick access to their store of live enzymes, vitamins and minerals. Unhindered by fibre, which needs to be digested, all the goodness in the juice goes straight into the bloodstream for instant effect. Fibre is important, though, and eating fibre-rich food and drinking fresh vegetable juice is an excellent recipe for a healthy, strong immune system.

Powerful ingredients such as beets, parsley, garlic, ginger and cayenne should be used in small doses until you become accustomed to them. Other juices such as celery and cucumber have a mild neutral flavour that makes a good base for ingredients with stronger flavours. Carrots add sweetness, balance and a creamy consistency.

All Green Vegetable Cocktail New!

This emerald cocktail is particularly delicious because of the kale, which adds sweetness to the flavour. Kale, an ancient member of the cabbage family, is an exceptional source of chlorophyll, calcium, folic acid, iron and vitamin A.

Ingredients

1 handful	green kale
10 stalks	parsley
6 stalks	celery
1	lemon, peeled
1	cucumber, whole

Method

Juice the kale first. Follow with the parsley, celery and lemon. Finish with the cucumber.

Beetroot Frappé Cocktail New!

The natural chlorine found in beet juice is an excellent cleanser of the liver, kidneys and gall bladder. Beets are known to be a valuable juice for toning the blood and feeding the red blood cells with a quality organic source of iron. The earthy flavour of beets is balanced by the sweetness of apples and carrots in this recipe.

Ingredients

1/2 inch	ginger root
1 small	beet, scrubbed
2 medium	red apples
3 medium	carrots
2 shakes	nutmeg
3	ice cubes

Method

Juice the ginger first. Follow with the beet and apples. Finish with the carrots. Transfer the vegetable juice to the blender. Start on a low setting while you add 2 shakes of nutmeg and the ice. Switch to a higher setting and blend briefly.

Refresher Cocktail (New!)

It's very important not to overdo the lemon in this vibrant cocktail so you can taste the rest of the ingredients, which are more subtle. The high silicon and sulphur content of the cucumber promotes strong nails, healthy hair and smooth elastic skin. Cucumber is also a natural diuretic.

Ingredients

1/2 inch	ginger root
1/2	lemon, peeled
1/2	cucumber
2 medium	red apples
3 medium	carrots

Method

Juice the ginger first. Follow with the lemon, cucumber and apples. Finish with the carrots.

Red Rocket Cocktail

"The Red Rocket" is slang for our public transportation system in Toronto. I named this as a metaphor for the speedy transport of vital nutrients throughout our bodies. A round-trip fare on the Red Rocket costs the same as a large glass of vegetable juice. By the way, fresh ginger juice has been proven beneficial in easing motion sickness, nausea and stomach aches.

Ingredients

1/2 inch	ginger root
1 small	beet, scrubbed
3 medium	carrots

Method

Juice the ginger first. Follow with the beet and finish with the carrots.

Spring Tonic Cocktail New!

The Spring Tonic is a light cleansing cocktail. The pectin in apples removes cholesterol and toxic metals such as lead and mercury. Apples promote good digestion. This is a good drink to have first thing in the morning to wake your body up.

Ingredients

2	red apples
1 handful	green kale
1/2	lemon, peeled
2	pink grapefruits

Method

Juice the kale first. Follow with the lemon and apples. Finish with the grapefruit.

Detox Cocktail

Believe it or not this cocktail is sweet, smooth and satisfying. You don't need to feel toxic to enjoy this drink. Raw spinach has properties necessary for the cleansing and regeneration of the intestinal tract. Rich in iron, magnesium, chlorophyll and sodium, this combination detoxifies and builds the blood. Sodium, found in celery, is one of the most important elements in the elimination of carbon dioxide from the system.

Ingredients

10 stalks	parsley
1 handful	spinach
3 stalks	celery
3 medium	carrots

Method

Juice the parsley first. Follow with the spinach. Continue with the celery and finish with the carrots.

Sweet Surrender Cocktail

When you are feeling low and depleted, surrender yourself to the gift of fresh organic carrot juice and I promise you will feel better. Carrot juice is my first love, and I still crave a simple glass despite the availability of so many other vegetable juices. The richest source of vitamin A (beta-carotene) with an ample supply of vitamins B, C, D, E, G and K, carrot juice is also very rich in the vital organic alkaline elements sodium and potassium. On top of that, it has a good supply of calcium, magnesium, iron, phosphorus, sulphur, silicon and chlorine.

Ingredients

1/2 inch	ginger root
2 medium	red apples
3 medium	carrots

Method

Juice the ginger first. Follow with the apples. Finish with the carrots.

Garden Cocktail

Every juice bar has a garden cocktail on the menu because people like to get all their vegetables and nutrition in one quick glass. However, if there are too many ingredients in one combination, you'll never get the proportions necessary for each ingredient to enjoy their benefits and uses. Less is more. Six ingredients maximum for a large glass of juice is a good limit.

Ingredients

1 handful	spinach
1 clove	garlic
1/2	beet, scrubbed
3 stalks	celery
3 medium	carrots

Method

Juice the spinach first. Follow with the garlic, beet and celery. Finish with the carrots.

Root Juice Cocktail

Parsnips, when juiced, have a creamy, sweet and nutty flavour that goes well with other root vegetables. I'm told that parsnips grow sweeter the longer they are left in the ground and the colder it gets. Parsnips are a good source of potassium, silicon, vitamin C and sulphur.

Ingredients

1/2 inch	ginger root
4 medium	parsnips
1 small	beet, scrubbed
3 medium	carrots

Method

Juice the ginger first. Follow with the parsnips and beet. Finish with the carrots.

Diablo Cocktail

The taste of red pepper and Stash's Hot Sauce make this cocktail special. Juicing red peppers enhances the wonderful flavour and aroma as much as roasting them. I love a spicy juice and I find this is a good one to have with a savoury dinner.

Ingredients

1 clove	garlic
1/2	lemon, peeled
1/2	red pepper
2 stalks	celery
3 medium	carrots
1/2 tsp.	Stash's Hot Sauce (see p. 95)

Method

Juice the garlic first. Follow with the lemon, red pepper and celery. Finish with the carrots. Stir in the hot sauce.

Flu Fighter Cocktail Hot

Garlic, rich in mustard oils and potassium, is said to be one of nature's most effective antibiotics. Its juice thins the blood, improves circulation and promotes sweating. Sweating is a good thing when you are trying to rid your body of unfriendly bacteria, toxins and viruses. Ginger is a source of zinc and copper, which have antiviral properties and work to promote a strong immune system. Cayenne pepper is one of the highest sources of botanic vitamin C. The lemon, apart from its own vitamin C content, lightens up the flavour of the juice and eases the heat of the cayenne.

Ingredients

1/2 inch	ginger root
1 clove	garlic
1 handful	spinach
1	lemon, peeled
3 stalks	celery
3 medium	carrots
1 shake	cayenne pepper

Method

Juice the ginger and garlic first. Follow with the spinach, lemon and celery. Finish with the carrots. Heat gently in a saucepan and add the cayenne. To preserve nutrients, be sure to remove the pan from the heat once juice is nice and warm, but well before it comes to a boil. Pour into a large mug. Sip slowly.

> Deep Immune Elixir 147
> Hot Apple Pie Smoothie 181

> Fresh on Spadina

Supplements and Herbal Tinctures

Supplements

Blending your supplements into juice ensures their easy and quick absorption. The supplements used at Fresh are in the form of loose powders, pastes or liquids. Powder, rather than pills or capsules, is more practical for blending into drinks. I match supplements with different tasty juice combinations. The following are my tried-and-true favourites. One tablespoon per serving of juice once a day is the recommended amount unless you are feeling especially depleted.

Chywanprash

Chywanprash is a 2,000-year-old recipe first documented by the ancient Indian sage Charaka. It is an Ayurvedic sweet and spicy paste of 49 plants, fruits, roots, herbs and minerals. Widely used in India as a daily immune enhancer, it has a high concentration of vitamin C. This sticky paste, available in most Indian food and spice shops, requires a blender for juice combinations unless you are drinking it hot. I like to drink it with fresh-cut ginger and hot apple cider. One tablespoon of paste per serving makes for a strong and deeply soothing drink.

Greens+

Greens+ is a blend of easily absorbed, nutrient-rich, concentrated superfoods. Superfoods are a potent source of plant-based vitamins, minerals, enzymes, cell salts, trace minerals, antioxidants and amino acids. At the foundation of Greens+ are the grasses of barley, wheat and alfalfa, as well as the algae spirulina, chlorella, dulse and dunaliella. As well, there are organically grown soy sprouts, antioxidant herbs and extracts, probiotic cultures and pectins, royal jelly, ginseng and 29 different herbs and superfoods. With steady use, Greens+ is reputed to increase energy, improve stamina, sharpen mental alertness and cleanse toxins in the blood. This chlorophyll cocktail is easy to mix without a blender and is by far the best-tasting one I've come across. Use one tablespoon per serving of juice once or twice a day. Greens+ and similar green drink supplements can be bought at most health food stores.

Hawaiian Spirulina

A blue-green micro-algae, spirulina is farmed organically in Hawaii and other parts of the world. Spirulina contains high doses of 10 readily assimilated essential nutrients: vitamin A (beta-carotene), vitamins B1, B2, B12, niacin, calcium, phosphorus, magnesium, iron and protein. These nutrients are most beneficial for stress-related mental and physical fatigue, for iron deficiency and as a super-protein boost. The high chlorophyll content builds and enriches the blood, detoxifies the kidneys and liver, and enhances intestinal flora. Spirulina is now widely available in health food stores. One tablespoon per serving of juice a day is sufficient. You will need a blender to mix this fine sticky powder.

Hemp, Sprouted Flax and Maca Protein

This is a low-carb, high-protein powder that contains all essential amino acids. The brand we use is called Ruth's. Raw hemp and sprouted flax seeds are rich in Omega 3 fatty acids, high-lignan fibre for improved health, plus essential fatty acids for the skin and heart. Organic maca is a nutritious root vegetable grown at high altitudes in Peru. Known to be rich in trace minerals, it is reputed to improve energy levels, mental clarity and focus. Athletes often use maca to boost energy and endurance. Hemp protein and maca protein powders are ingredients that can easily be found separately at most health food stores these days. Combine them yourself to make a powerful vegan protein mix.

Matcha Green Tea

Matcha is made from the top three youngest leaves of the green tea plant, carefully ground into a fine powder that contains a high concentration of antioxidants, immune-boosting catechins and the brain stimulant L theanine. It is reputed to support healthy blood sugar levels, increase metabolism, lower cholesterol and blood pressure. Matcha is 10 times stronger than a regular cup of brewed green tea. Drinking matcha is an ancient Japanese tea ritual often reserved for royalty.

Spirutein

Spirutein is a soy-based protein powder that contains spirulina, oat bran, apple pectin, bee pollen, enzymes, vitamins and minerals. This yeast-free product promotes internal cleansing using fibre-rich ingredients. I like to use the banana-flavoured Spirutein. It produces a rich, creamy drink that is also filling. There are many other excellent soy protein products on the shelves today, but check the ingredients carefully. I avoid sugars, preservatives, whey powders, dairy products and ingredients I don't recognize that have more than six letters. Use one tablespoon per serving of juice a day. You will need a blender for this protein supplement.

Vitamin C / Ascorbic Acid

Vitamin C plays a vital role in strengthening the immune system, especially with regard to preventing and treating the common cold. Vitamin C has been shown to be antiviral and antibacterial. At Fresh, we use the ascorbic acid loose powder in our drinks instead of sodium ascorbate, which has a salty flavour that is not suitable for juices. Ascorbic acid vitamin C can be easily found in your local vitamin and supplements store or health food store. Ascorbic acid has a tangy flavour that goes great in fruit or vegetable juice and blends easily without a blender. Use a half teaspoon per serving of juice once or twice a day.

Wheat Germ

Wheat germ is part of the outer layer of the wheat kernel. It is rich in B vitamins, vitamin E and minerals. It has a high fibre content and is a good-quality protein. Store it in a cool, dry place and eat it as fresh as possible. Use one tablespoon per serving of juice a day.

Wheatgrass

Plants, through the process of photosynthesis, convert the sun's energy to produce chlorophyll and then release oxygen into the atmosphere. When we "drink our greens" we are taking in the sun's energy, which gives life to all living things on this planet. Fresh-pressed wheatgrass is precious, potent and intense in flavour and effect. In the juicing world, wheatgrass is considered the crème de la crème of all juices. Wheatgrass is young sprouted wheat berries grown indoors on trays in enriched soil. Nutritional scientists have hailed it as the most powerful blood, tissue and colon cleanser. As it detoxifies the liver and kidneys, it enriches and builds the blood with an array of vitamins and minerals. One or two ounces of wheatgrass a day helps maintain a strong and healthy immune system. Juicing the fine blades of wheatgrass requires a specific juicer. If you don't have a juicer for juicing fresh-cut wheatgrass, you can buy it flash-frozen by the ounce or in capsule or powder form.

Herbal Tinctures

Herbal tinctures are high-concentration herbal extracts preserved in grain-based alcohol or water. Taken in liquid form, the active ingredients of these potent herbs are absorbed and assimilated into the body quickly and efficiently. Herbal pills or capsules, which can also contain fillers and binders, have to be broken down and digested before the body can benefit from their properties.

For maximum absorption into the bloodstream, take herbal tinctures in water, juice or non-caffeinated tea and not at meal times. This could mean taking them right when you get up, at mid-morning or mid-afternoon, or just before you go to sleep. Golden seal, licorice root and osha root should be avoided during pregnancy and when breast-feeding.

Herbal tinctures are available in most health food stores. Royal jelly, panax ginseng and gingko biloba are all items you can also find in your local Chinese herbal pharmacy.

Echinacea

Echinacea is an herb that was used extensively by Native Americans to combat illness and infections and as an antidote for rattlesnake bites.

It was also used externally for the healing of wounds, burns and abscesses. This herbal extract mobilizes the immune system response to bacterial invaders by increasing the production and aggressiveness of white blood cells. Echinacea quickly eliminates waste products by stimulating lymphatic drainage and helps the body regain its balance. Echinacea is most effective when taken at the first signs of a cold or flu.

Gingko Biloba

Gingko comes from an ancient family of Japanese trees that can live more than 2,500 years. Gingko biloba is an antioxidant-rich herb that has a scavenging effect on free radicals. It increases dopamine, which aids in memory retention and mental alertness. Extracts of gingko biloba have been shown to increase the flow of blood and oxygen to the brain, easing dizziness, ringing of the ears and poor circulation. It has been beneficial to musicians, especially drummers, concerned about the effects of really loud music on their hearing.

Goldenseal and Echinacea

The combination of these two extracts is helpful once you are in battle with the cold or flu. Goldenseal liquifies mucus and reduces inflammation of the throat, sinuses and bronchial tissues. Echinacea and goldenseal assist in breaking fevers and stimulating the immune system's response. Echinacea quickly eliminates waste products by stimulating lymphatic drainage and helps the body regain its balance.

Licorice Root

Licorice root is an adrenal gland booster. It has mild anti-inflammatory and anti-histaminic properties to provide relief for sore throats and coughs. Do not use when pregnant.

Milk Thistle

The ultimate healing herb for the liver, milk thistle is a stout biennial plant, found in dry rocky soils in southern and western Europe and some parts of the United States. The seeds, fruit and leaves are used for medicinal purposes. Milk thistle detoxifies the liver, protects it from harmful substances and promotes its regeneration.

Osha Root

Osha root is a North American perennial herb from the parsley family. The root, being the most potent part of the osha, is the most widely used. Osha root helps loosen phlegm, soothe sore throats and is an effective treatment for viral colds and flu. Do not use when pregnant.

Panax Chinese Red Ginseng

Panax ginseng is a small perennial plant that originally grew wild in the damp woodlands of northern China, Manchuria and Korea. Chinese ginseng root extract, considered the most stimulating of all the ginsengs, has been harvested and used by Chinese people for centuries. Panax ginseng is used to aid recovery from illness, to relieve stress and fatigue, and to improve mental and physical performance, stamina and endurance.

Royal Jelly

Royal jelly is produced by nurse bees who chew pollen and mix it with secretions from their glands. It is then fed to infant bees and is the sole food of the queen bee. Keep in mind that this tonic is an animal by-product and a tremendous amount of energy is spent making it. Royal jelly may be taken by those in need of rich animal nutrition who prefer not to eat meat. It is a well-known booster of immune functions and is rich in protein, vitamins and enzymes. Premium-quality royal jelly is a super-nutrient containing vitamins A, C, D and E as well as nine B complex vitamins. It also contains 22 amino acids and notable quantities of the minerals calcium, copper, iron, potassium, magnesium and sulphur.

Glossary

The following items are commonly available at most natural food stores and specialty food markets.

Apple Cider Vinegar

The best kind of apple cider vinegar is the naturally brewed unfiltered type made from whole organic apples. Apple cider vinegar has an abundance of potassium and also contains malic acid, an element involved in the process of digestion. Whereas white vinegar is acidic and harmful, apple cider vinegar is alkaline and soothing to the system.

Balsamic Vinegar

A mellow, dark brown Italian vinegar made from the white Trebbiano grape.

Brown Basmati Rice

An unhulled long-grain Indian rice with a delicious nutty flavour. This lightly textured rice works well with heavier sauces and curries.

Chipotle Peppers

Chipotle chili peppers are sold canned in Latino grocery stores and some supermarkets. Chipotles are smoked, red, spicy jalapeño peppers that have a subtle Southwestern flavour.

Durum Flour

A hard whole wheat flour most often used to make pasta products. Whole wheat berries ground into flour add a mild nutty flavour to baked goods and are used as a base for sauces.

Engevita (inactive) Yeast

A dried yeast that is inactive and will not raise bread. It is a valuable source of vitamin B, which, in powdered or flaked form, may be sprinkled over food or used in recipes. It has a pungent flavour that is similar to cheese.

Lemongrass

Lemon-scented stalks of grass used in Thai cooking. The stalks are tough, so peel the outer leaves away and use the tender inside part at the end of each stalk. Remove the lemongrass before serving.

Maple Syrup

The boiled-down sap of the sugar maple tree that is used as a natural sweetener. Grade C maple syrup is the least processed and ranks highest in mineral content.

Mirin Rice Wine

Mirin is a sweet rice wine used as a seasoning and sweetener. During cooking, the alcohol evaporates, leaving a glaze and distinct flavour. Great for glazing tofu or vegetables in the wok.

Miso

A fermented soybean paste popular in Japanese cooking. Miso, pungent and salty, can also be made with brown rice or barley. The blond and red misos are milder than the dark brown misos, which are stronger in flavour. Use in miso soup and miso gravy.

Sea Salt

A natural rock salt not subjected to heat, chemical processes or additives as is regular table salt.

Soba Noodles

Japanese noodles made from buckwheat flour with a delicate nut-like flavour. Buckwheat is not a grain but the seeds of the plant known as Saracen corn. Rich in B vitamins, soba noodles are a popular alternative for people with wheat allergies.

Soymilk

A non-dairy milk made from soybeans. Many brands are available on the market. The original flavour is most commonly used for cooking. Use as a substitute for cow's milk in recipes.

Spelt Flour

A relative of wheat, spelt is considered one of the original ancient grains farmed in the Middle East more than 9,000 years ago. People with allergies to wheat or gluten generally do not have reactions to spelt. Spelt is a hearty grain with a thick, protective husk and a nutty flavour. It is higher in protein, fat and fibre than most varieties of wheat.

Tahini

A raw sesame butter or paste used in Middle Eastern cooking. This thick paste is made from ground-up sesame seeds and is used as a base for hummus and tahini sauce.

Tamari

Tamari is a naturally fermented soy sauce made without chemicals and preservatives. Soy sauce is made from a mixture of wheat and soybeans, water and sea salt. Low-sodium and wheat-free tamari is also available. Use as a substitute for soy sauce or salt.

Tempeh

A fermented high-protein product, traditionally used in Indonesia, made from whole soybeans with a nutty flavour and meaty texture. Great for grilling.

Toasted Nori

A delicate and tasty sea vegetable dried and pressed flat into paper-thin sheets and toasted. Use in nori rolls, rice bowls, soups and sushi.

Tofu

Tofu is a soybean curd made from soymilk. Extremely versatile and mild tasting, it is used often in vegetarian and Asian cooking. It has a custard-like texture that easily absorbs the flavours of other foods. Tofu is an excellent source of vegetable protein.

Umeboshi Plum Paste

This prepared paste is made from the purple umeboshi salt plum. Highly alkalizing, umeboshi salt plums are good for treating indigestion and are sometimes called Japanese Alka-Seltzer. A thin layer is spread on the rice for sushi or nori rolls.

Vegan

An animal-free diet that excludes all meat, fish, fowl, dairy and eggs. This also includes animal by-products such as butter, honey, royal jelly, bee pollen and gelatin.

Wasabi

Also known as Japanese horseradish. The green root of a plant ground into a fine powder and mixed with water to make a thin paste.

> Fresh on Spadina

Bibliography

Calbom, Cherie, and Maureen Keane. *Juicing for Life*. New York: Avery Publishing Group Inc., 1992.

Diamond, Harvey. *You Can Prevent Breast Cancer*. San Diego: Pro Motion Publishing, 1995.

Gagnon, Daniel J. *Liquid Herbal Drops for Everyday Use*. Santa Fe: Botanical Research & Education Institute Inc., 1996.

Graci, Sam. *The Power of Superfoods*. Scarborough: Prentice Hall Canada Inc., 1997.

Gentry, Ann. *The Real Food Daily Cookbook*. Berkeley: Ten Speed Press, 2005.

Lappé, Anna, and Bryant Terry. *Grub: Ideas for an Urban Organic Kitchen*. New York: Penguin Group (USA), 2006.

Marquand, Ed. *Smoothies and Juices*. New York: Abbeville Press Publishers, 1998.

Meyerowitz, Steve. *Food Combining and Digestion*. Great Barrington, MA: The Sprout House Inc., 1987.

Meyerowitz, Steve. *Nature's Finest Medicine*. Great Barrington, MA: Sproutman Publications, 1998.

Murray, Michael T. *Natural Alternatives to Over-the-Counter Prescription Drugs*. New York: William Morrow and Company, Inc.,1994.

Murray, Michael, and Joseph Pizzorno, *Encyclopaedia of Natural Medicine*. London: Little Brown and Company, 1990.

Pitchford, Paul. *Healing with Whole Foods: Oriental Traditions and Modern Nutrition*. Berkeley: North Atlantic Books, 1993.

Robbins, John. *Diet for a New America*. Walpole, NH: Still Point Publishing, 1987.

Safford, Julie. *Juicing for Life*. Boston: Charles E. Tuttle Company Inc., 1994.

Tucker, Eric, and John Westerdahl. *The Millennium Cookbook*. Berkeley: Ten Speed Press, 1998.

Walker, Norman. *Fresh Fruit and Vegetable Juices*. What's Missing in Your Body? Prescott, AZ: Norwalk Press, 1970.

Wigmore, Ann. *The Wheatgrass Book*. Wayne, NJ: Avery Publishing Group, 1985.

Recipe Index

General Index